Modern
Basketball
Team
Techniques

Also by the Author:

Basketball's Pro-Set Playbook: The Complete Offensive
    Arsenal
Basketball's Stack Offense
Complete Book of Zone Game Basketball
Flex Continuity Basketball Offense
Modern Basketball Team Techniques
Pressure Game Defense

Modern Basketball Team Techniques

Harry L. "Mike" Harkins

PARKER PUBLISHING COMPANY
West Nyack, New York 10994

Library of Congress Cataloging-in-Publication Data

Harkins, Harry L.
   Modern basketball team techniques.
   Includes index.
   ISBN 0-13-587908-6
   1. Basketball—Coaching. I. Title.
  GV885.3.H355 1985   85-9342
  796.32'32   CIP

Printed in the United States of America

10 9 8

ISBN 0-13-587908-6

PARKER PUBLISHING COMPANY
West Nyack, NY 10994

A Simon & Schuster Company

On the World Wide Web at http://www.phdirect.com

Prentice-Hall International (UK) Limited, *London*
Prentice-Hall of Australia Pty. Limited, *Sydney*
Prentice-Hall Canada Inc., *Toronto*
Prentice-Hall Hispanoamericana, S.A., *Mexico*
Prentice-Hall of India Private Limited, *New Delhi*
Prentice-Hall of Japan, Inc., *Tokyo*
Simon & Schuster Asia Pte. Ltd., *Singapore*
Editora Prentice-Hall do Brasil, Ltda., *Rio de Janeiro*

Dedication

This book is dedicated to my wife, Grace, who, along with being the love of my life, has been a working partner in the books I have written. Without her meticulous efforts on the diagrams and hours spent typing, they might never have been completed.

Acknowledgments

Grateful appreciation is expressed to the sources of my basketball knowledge, including:

Russ Estey and Mike Krino, my high school coaches.
Russ Beichly and Red Cochrane, my college coaches.
Buck Hyser, who gave me my first coaching job.
And the players who have played on my teams.

A final note of thanks goes to my number-one fans (and granddaughters) Shellee Ann and Jamee Cameron Harkins.

What This Book Will Do for You

The body of knowledge in the sport of basketball is increasing at a very rapid rate. Defensively, a coach must design techniques that not only counter the opposition's offensive plans, but attempt to dictate the tempo of the game. This may include man-to-man defenses that have evolved from simple "stay between your man and the basket" rules to intricate team plans that rotate, pressure and help, help and recover, run and jump, trap, fan, fade, influence, and make innumerable other gyrations. Zone defenses have not escaped this period of change and they now match, trap, rotate, flex, adjust, and even extend to full-court to become pressure defenses. As a coach, you must also present offensive plans that permit your team to compete successfully against them. This book attempts to simplify your job by: (A) Introducing you to some modern, mechanically sound team techniques; and (B) pointing out relationships in the various elements of team techniques, and how they can be combined or integrated.

The book progresses in the following manner: The first two chapters provide man-to-man offenses that may be adapted to face zone defenses. The offense in Chapter 1 is *The Multipurpose Double-Down Continuity* offense. It is based on set plays that culminate in a continuity. The offense in Chapter 2 is the *Three-Man Passing Game*. It relies on three rules that lead to many play situations.

Chapter 3, *Winning Zone Offense,* begins with the fundamentals of a zone plan. This is followed by seven zone offensive series. A coach may adopt one of the series as his zone offense or integrate parts of several into his present plan.

Chapter 4, *An Offensive Full-Court Traffic Pattern,* offers a novel pattern that may be used when: The opposition fails to score and you want to fast break from a missed field goal; the opposition fails to score and you want to fast break from a missed free throw; the opposition scores and applies a full-court zone press; when the opposition scores and applies man-to-man pressure.

Chapter 5 is entitled *Defeating the Zone Press*. It includes four innovative zone-pressure offensive plans.

Chapter 6, *Ball-Control Techniques,* is designed to enable your team to practice a disciplined ball-control game and develop fastidious shot selection. It features four offenses that attempt to make the opposition spend a great deal of time on defense.

Chapter 7 is *Versatile Out-of-Bounds Plays.* Coaching strategy and rule changes have increased the importance of this phase of the game. This chapter provides inbounding methods from all areas of the court, and prepares your team to meet the situations that demand them.

Chapter 8, *The Hybrid Man-to-Man Defense,* combines the two major widely accepted man-to-man defensive theories to offer an airtight, comprehensive defensive plan.

Chapter 9, *Zoning with Man-to-Man Principles,* permits you to utilize a defensive plan that combines the strengths of both zone and man-to-man defenses.

Chapter 10, *Applying Zone Pressure,* starts with some basic assumptions that may increase the chances of success for any zone pressure defense. It then provides several pressure defenses designed to counter modern zone-pressure offensive plans.

I feel this text may help you in either of two ways. First, you may adopt one or more of these ideas, and benefit from the extra practice time they provide by simplifying and combining the elements of team techniques. This simplification of techniques may occur in many ways including using one of the offenses against man-to-man, zone, or combination defenses; utilizing the zone defense based on man-to-man principles, adopting the man-to-man defense that utilizes zone methods, trying the zone-press offense that may be used versus both half-court and full-court defenses; or attempting one of the suggested man-to-man out-of-bounds plays that are adaptable to zone defenses. Second, you may choose to maintain your present team techniques, but take a look at them in terms of their adaptability and use in other situations. The result may be a saving of valuable practice time, and an improvement in the teaching and learning environment of your practice situation. Whatever the effect, I hope that through this work I have made some contribution to your success in the often frustrating, but always challenging and invigorating profession of coaching basketball.

Mike Harkins

Contents

Multipurpose Double-Down Continuity Offense

one

The double-down offense is a continuity offense that may be run against man-to-man, zone, and combination defenses. It is a power offense because its primary scoring options are based on the inside game. The continuity is always preceded by a pattern set play. A pattern set play is a simple maneuver that may or may not contain a scoring option. However, when it concludes, the personnel are in position to run the basic pattern. By using this device, a simple pattern may be given variety. It is also functional as the season progresses to meet specific situations, or to take advantage of particular match-ups.

PERSONNEL ALIGNMENT

The offense is run from a two-guard set. Although the plays may be initiated on either side, player (1) is the lead guard and will start most of them. Player (2) may be a defensive specialist and will very often have the task of maintaining defensive balance. Forwards (3) and (4), and post man (5), are the inside men and, for the most part, are interchangeable. This, plus the fact that the post man must set up high, negates the necessity for a very tall post player. See Diagram 1-1.

Following is a wide variety of pattern set plays. You should select two or three that are most compatible with your offensive

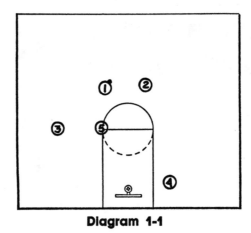

Diagram 1-1

philosophy and the personnel available to you. As the season progresses, you may change pattern set plays or add to those you have chosen initially.

THE UCLA CUT PLAY

In Diagram 1-2, the basic UCLA cut is run with guard (1) passing to his forward (3) and making a slash cut off post man (5) to the ball-side low-post area.

Player (5) then steps out, and (3) passes to him. Player (3) screens down for (1), who pops out to the ball-side wing area. At the same time, forward (4) steps up and screens for (2). Guard (2) cuts to the offside wing position. See Diagram 1-3.

Player (5) may then pass to (1) popping out; (2), at the off-side wing; (3) in the ball-side low post; or to (4) rolling to the basket after his screen for (2). See Diagram 1-4.

When (5) passes to either wing, it keys the double-down continuity. In Diagram 1-5, (5) passes to (1). This starts the continuity and tells (3) to screen away for (4), who cuts to the ball-side low-post position. The offside wing man (2) hesitates one count and then moves to the high-post area. See Diagram 1-6.

The wing man's movement creates a dilemma for X4, the defender on (4). If he plays (4) in a three-quarter defensive position, a pass to (2) will leave the offensive low-post man (4) inside X4 for an easy power lay-up shot. See Diagram 1-7.

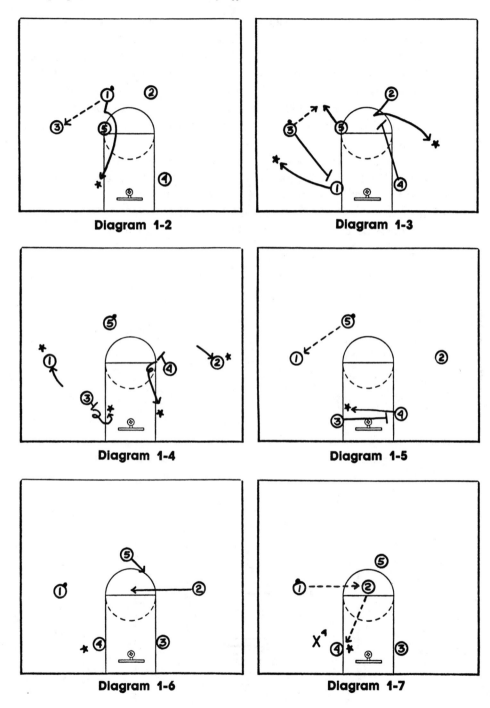

Diagram 1-2

Diagram 1-3

Diagram 1-4

Diagram 1-5

Diagram 1-6

Diagram 1-7

4 *Multipurpose Double-Down Continuity Offense*

If X4 chooses to play behind (4), the result is a one-on-one play in the low-post area which is very difficult to defend.

If X4 chooses to front (4), he is vulnerable to a lob pass because the next phase of the continuity is for (2) and (5) to come down and screen for (3), who pops to the point. This means that for an instant, the primary offside helper X3 is too involved in fighting over the double-down screen to be of any help to (4). See Diagram 1-8.

If (4) is not open, (1) passes to (3). After that, (1) screens down for (4) and (2) loops around (5). Players (4) and (2) pop to their respective wing areas (Diagram 1-9). Once (3) passes to either wing (as to (2) in Diagram 1-10), the double-down continuity pattern is repeated. See Diagrams 1-10 through 1-13.

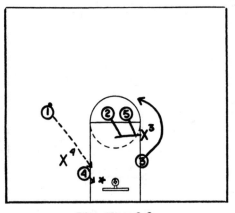

Diagram 1-8

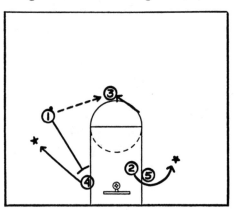

Diagram 1-9

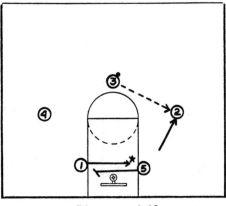

Diagram 1-10

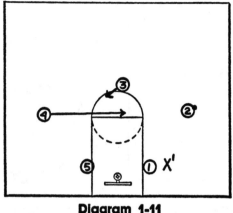

Diagram 1-11

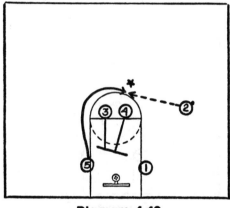

Diagram 1-12

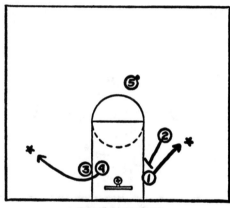

Diagram 1-13

THE LOB-CUT PLAY

This time when (1) passes to his forward (3), the offside forward (4) swings to the ball-side low-post area. This permits (1) to cut off of (5) to the offside lay-up slot for a possible lob pass from (3). See Diagram 1-14.

If (1) is not open for the lob pass, (5) again steps out and receives a pass from (3). Player (3) then screens down for (4), and (2) (who drifted to the wing on (1)'s pass to (3)) screens down for (1). See Diagram 1-15.

As soon as (5) passes to either wing, the double-down continuity is run. See Diagrams 1-16 and 1-17.

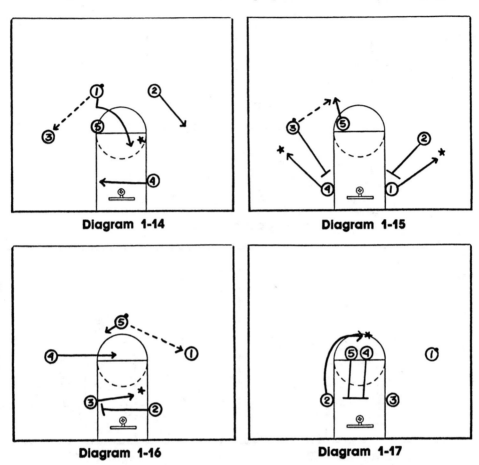

Diagram 1-14

Diagram 1-15

Diagram 1-16

Diagram 1-17

THE DICK MOTTA DIAGONAL PLAY

The Diagonal Play was made popular by Coach Motta's Chicago Bull teams. In this case, however, it is used for a pattern set maneuver.

In Diagram 1-18, guard (1) passes to his forward (3), and then cuts diagonally down the lane to screen for the offside forward (4). Player (4) cuts to the head of the key, (2) drifts to the

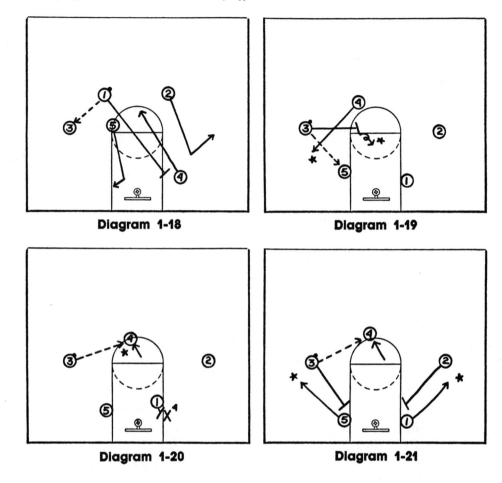

Diagram 1-18

Diagram 1-19

Diagram 1-20

Diagram 1-21

offside wing area, and post man (5) swings to the ball-side low-post area.

In Coach Motta's system, (3) could pass to (5) and split the post with (4) (see Diagram 1-19), or simply pass to (4) who would look for a jump shot. See Diagram 1-20.

The pass to the low post and eventual split play is a viable option. However, in this context, when (3) passes to (4), it initiates two downscreens, with (3) screening down for (5) and (2) screening down for (1). See Diagram 1-21.

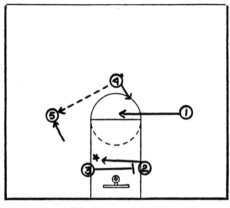

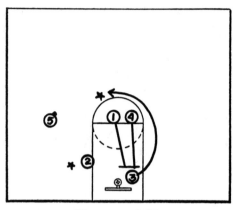

Diagram 1-22   **Diagram 1-23**

Once (4) passes to either wing, it leads to the double-down continuity. See Diagrams 1-22 and 1-23.

PASS-TO-THE-POST PLAY

In order to take the defensive pressure off forward (3), (1) passes to post man (5). Forward (3) then backdoors his over-playing defender X3 for a possible lay-up shot. See Diagram 1-24.

Note in the above diagram that (1), after passing to (5), splits the high-post with (2). If (3) is not open, he stops and (1) loops down and around the offside forward (4). Guard (2) moves down to screen for (3) who pops out on the ball side. See Diagram 1-25.

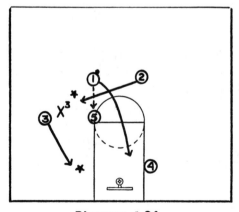

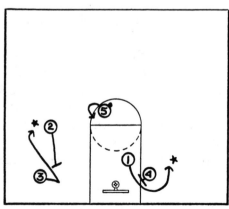

Diagram 1-24   **Diagram 1-25**

Player (5) may then pass to either wing and the double-down continuity will follow.

THE DRIBBLE-ENTRY PLAY

Three variations of the dribble-entry play may be run from this formation as pattern set maneuvers for the double-down continuity. They are:

A. Forward (3) clear away

B. Forward (3) clear to corner

C. Forward (3) clear high

A. Forward Clear Away

In Diagram 1-26, guard (1) dribbles at forward (3) and clears him away and across the lane. This keys post-man (5) to screen away for guard (2) who cuts the ball-side lay-up slot.

Guard (1) looks first for guard (2). If (2) is not open, post man (5) pops to the head of the key and (1) passes to him. Then (1) screens down for (2) and (3) loops around (4). See Diagrams 1-27 and 1-28.

Player (5) will then pass to either wing and the double-down continuity will ensue.

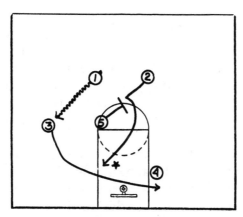

Diagram 1-26

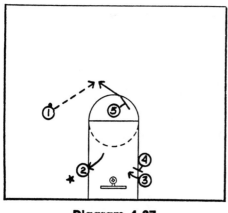 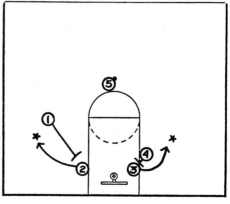

Diagram 1-27   **Diagram 1-28**

B. Forward Clear to Corner

This time, when (1) dribbles at (3), he ((3)) clears to the ball-side corner. Post man (5) again screens away for (2), who cuts to the ball-side low-post area. See Diagram 1-29.

If guard (2) is not open, (5) steps out and receives a pass from (1). See Diagram 1-30. When this happens, guard (1) screens down for (3) and (2) crosses the lane to loop around (4). See Diagram 1-31.

Player (5) may then pass to either wing and the double-down continuity will follow.

C. Forward Clear High

In Diagram 1-32, guard (1) again dribbles at (3) who this time clears to the head of the key. Guard (2) uses this cut and (5)'s position to move out to the ball-side low-post area.

If (2) is not open, he clears across the lane to stack under (4). Post man (5) rolls to the ball-side low-post position. See Diagram 1-33.

Player (1) checks (5) in the low-post area, then passes to (3) at the head of the key (Diagram 1-34). This keys (1) to screen down for (5) and (4) to screen down for (2). Forward (3) then passes to either wing and the double-down continuity is in operation. See Diagram 1-35.

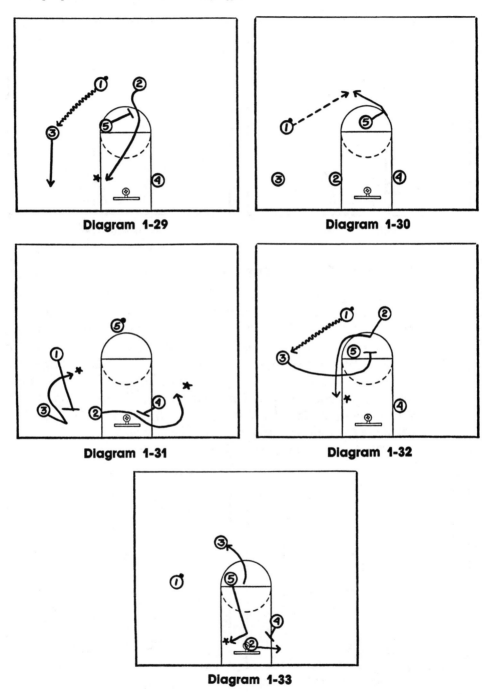

Diagram 1-29

Diagram 1-30

Diagram 1-31

Diagram 1-32

Diagram 1-33

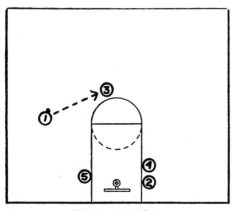

Diagram 1-34

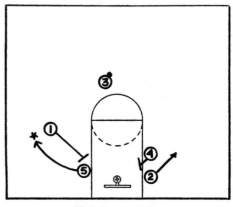

Diagram 1-35

The Wing-Denial Option

Along with using the dribble entry as a pattern set maneuver, you may also use it during the continuity as a pressure reliever. As the season progresses, many teams will attempt to deny the point-to-wing pass that characterizes the double-down pattern. When this occurs, the point man ((5) in Diagram 1-36) dribbles at wing man (3), and clears him to the offside-wing area. The former offside wing man ((2)) breaks to the point and receives a quick pass from (5). Player (5) then screens down for (4), and (3) loops around (1). See Diagram 1-37.

The continuity is then back on track.

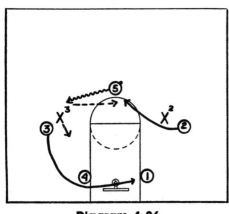

Diagram 1-36

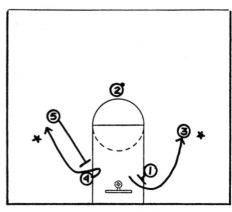

Diagram 1-37

DOUBLE-DOWN VERSUS THE ZONE DEFENSE

The secret to using this system versus zone defenses is the fact that the basic double-down continuity is an excellent zone offense.

Versus zones, it is best keyed by either of two pattern set plays: the UCLA Entry Play, or the Dribble-Entry Clear-to-the-Corner Play.

The UCLA Entry Play

In Diagram 1-38, guard (1) passes to forward (3) and makes his slash cut off post man (5). Against zones, (1) cuts all the way to the ball-side corner and creates an overload. This cut also changes the offensive perimeter from a two-man front to a one-man front.

This overload continues and the triangles it forms are utilized until (5) steps to the ball-side point and receives a pass from (3). This movement tells (3) to screen down for (1) and attempt to trap the zone inside as (1) moves to the wing. At the same time, player (4) moves high and (2) cuts to the offside wing as per their man-to-man assignments. See Diagram 1-39.

At this point, it must be remembered that player (5) is a tall man and may be able to pass over the small front-zone men. Player (5)'s height would permit him to pass directly to (3) or (4) inside the zone. However, the basic plan is to initiate the

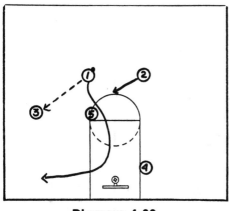

Diagram 1-38

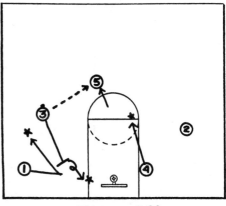

Diagram 1-39

double-down continuity so (5) passes to a wing man (as to (1) in Diagram 1-40). This pass tells (3) to screen away for (4) who cuts to the ball-side. See Diagram 1-41.

From here, timing is very important. Guard (2) must hesitate a count and then cut to the high-post area. If (1) passes to (2), (2) turns and looks for a shot or (if the defensive middleman of the zone moves up) for forwards (3) or (4) inside the zone. See Diagram 1-42.

If (1) cannot get the ball to (2), player (5) moves down and he and (2) form a double screen for (3) who loops to the point (Diagram 1-43). Guard (1) then passes to (3), and the pattern is repeated with the scoring options in mind. See Diagrams 1-44 through 1-48.

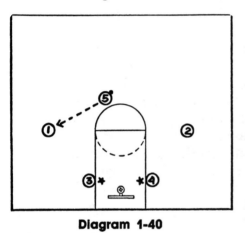

Diagram 1-40

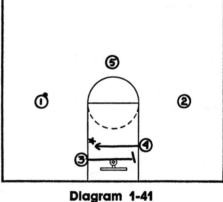

Diagram 1-41

Diagram 1-42

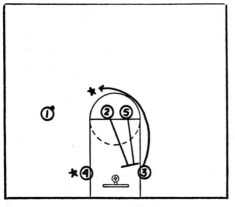

Diagram 1-43

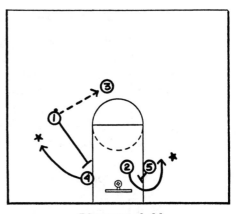

Diagram 1-44
Trap the Zone Inside

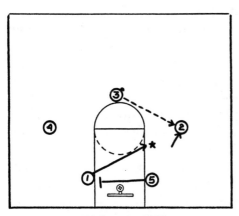

Diagram 1-45
Low-post Exchange

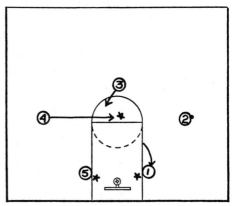

Diagram 1-46
Test the Middle

Diagram 1-47
Trap the Zone Inside

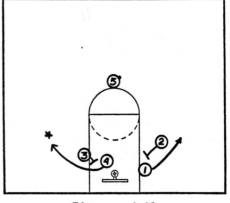

Diagram 1-48
Start Over

The Dribble-Entry Clear-to-the-Corner Play

In Diagram 1-49, (1) dribbles at his forward (3), who chooses to clear to the ball-side corner. Post man (5) then screens away for (2) who cuts to the ball-side post area. After screening, (5) pops to the point.

The result of this motion is a zone overload. Players (1), (5), (2), and (3) utilize the triangles formed by the overload by moving the ball and forcing the zone to shift. See Diagram 1-50.

Only player (1) may cancel the overload. He does this by passing to (5) at the point and screening down for (3) in the corner. The pass and screen tells (2) to move across the key and loop around (4). This motion restarts the basic continuity and cancels the overload. See Diagram 1-51.

This plan gives a team the ability to utilize a zone overload in the context of the continuity.

The combination of these two plays allows a team to test the zone's two most vulnerable areas—the corner and the high middle. The zone is overloaded, overshifted, and trapped inside. The fact that these plays may be run against zone or man-to-man defenses also makes them functional against combination and/or changing defenses.

I personally feel it is wise to start the season with three pattern set plays: The UCLA Cut Play, the Lob-Cut Play, and the

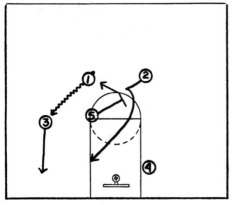

Diagram 1-49

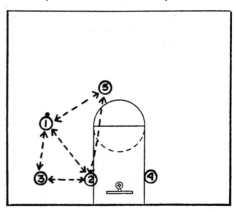

Diagram 1-50

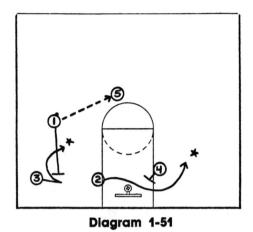

Diagram 1-51

Dribble-Entry Clear-to-the-Corner Play. This provides a well-coordinated offensive plan to successfully meet all types of defenses. As the season progresses, other pattern set plays and options may be added to meet specific situations or simply give depth to the offense. The double-down continuity provides the stability that would make this offensive plan easy to teach and, more importantly, easy to learn.

The Three-Man
Passing Game

two

In 1978, my book *Pressure Game Basketball* had a chapter on the three-man passing game. I felt at that time that it was the offense of the future. Since that time, I have developed a set of rules that simplify the teaching of this offense, and improve its efficiency. Following is an explanation of the offense built around three basic rules.

PERSONNEL ALIGNMENT

The offense consists of three motion players, (1), (2), and (3), that we call "movers." They initiate the offense. Player (1)

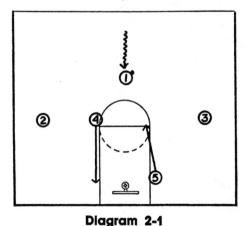

Diagram 2-1

assumes the point and players (2) and (3) play the wings. Big men (4) and (5) alternate at the high- and low-post positions. See Diagram 2-1.

THE THREE BASIC RULES

Rule 1—Mover-to-Mover Pass

When a mover passes to another mover, he screens away for the third mover. See (1)'s pass to (2) and screen for (3). As (3) receives the screen, he may use it and come toward the ball, as shown in Diagram 2-2, or cut away in an attempt to rub off a post man. When the latter occurs, the screener (1) pops back toward the ball (Diagram 2-3). Player (1), the screener, must read (3)'s cut and act accordingly.

Rule 2—Mover-to-Post Pass

When a mover, (1) in Diagram 2-4, passes to a post man ((4)), he screens for another mover ((2)) and the resulting cuts amount to a split of the post. The third mover, which in this case is (3), is free to make any cut to get open. This time he cuts off low-post man (5).

Note in the previous diagram that (4), after receiving the pass from (1), turned and looked inside for post man (5). Very often, (3)'s cut off (5) will force a switch and leave big man (5) being guarded by small man X3.

This play may also be initiated by low-post man (5) breaking to the high post and receiving a pass from (1). When this happens, (4) moves to the low-post. See Diagram 2-5.

If, after these cuts, no one is open, (5) will pass the ball to a perimeter mover and he will key another play. See Diagram 2-6.

Rule 3—The "Five Play"

Whenever all three movers are on the same side of the court (see Diagram 2-6), both post men ((4) and (5)) will cut to that side.

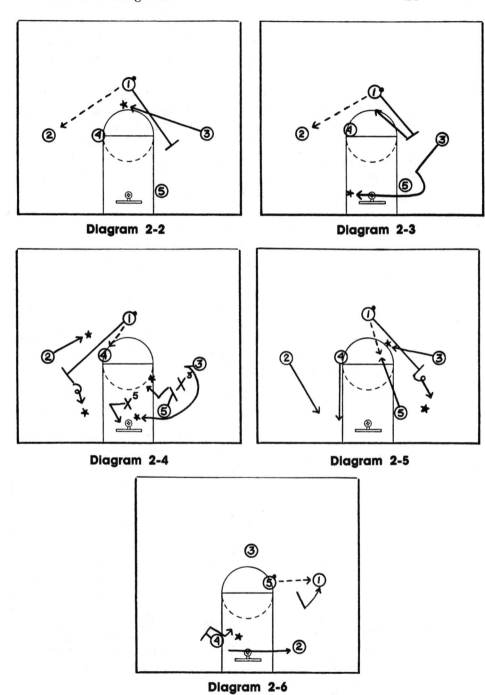

Diagram 2-2

Diagram 2-3

Diagram 2-4

Diagram 2-5

Diagram 2-6

For example: In Diagram 2-7, mover (1) passed to (2) and screened away for (3). Mover (3) chose not to use the screen and cut low off (5) and to the ball-side. Also note that (1) popped back to the ball.

Since (3) did not receive a pass from (2), he continued to the ball-side corner. Noting that all three movers were on the ball-side, post man (5) also cut to that area. See Diagram 2-8.

We call this alignment the "five-play set" and encourage the wing man with the ball to pass to either post man, (4) or (5). Once the pass is made to a post man, "Rule 2" is followed and the following play situations may result:

A. Mover (2) may pass to post man (4) and screen for (3) in the corner. This play makes (1) the third mover, who may cut to the basket. See Diagram 2-9.

B. Mover (2) may pass to (4) and screen for (1) at the point. This play keys (3) to cut to the basket. See Diagram 2-10.

   Very often when (3) cuts off of (5), a switch will occur and (5) can receive a pass from (4) for an easy power lay-up. See Diagram 2-11.

C. Mover (2) may pass to (5) and screen for (1). This play makes (3) the third mover and cutter. See Diagram 2-12.

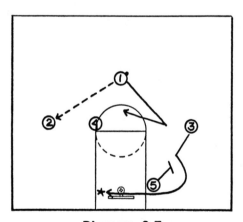

Diagram 2-7

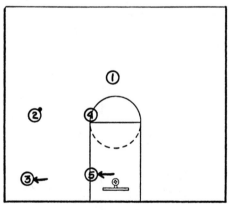

Diagram 2-8

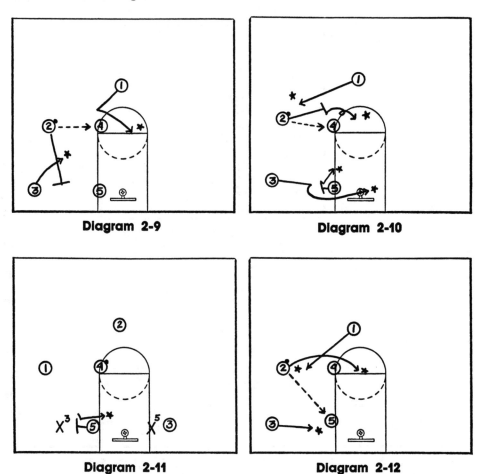

Diagram 2-9

Diagram 2-10

Diagram 2-11

Diagram 2-12

D. Mover (2) may pass to (5) and screen for (3). This play makes (1) the cutter. See Diagram 2-13.

E. Mover (2) may simply choose to pass to another mover and continue the motion. See Diagram 2-14.

Note that after screening, (2) moved to the offside wing to balance the offense. This move told (5) the "Five Play" was off and to move to his original position. See Diagram 2-15.

These three simple rules can lead to a myriad of play situations.

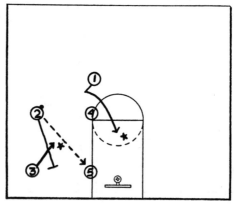

Diagram 2-13

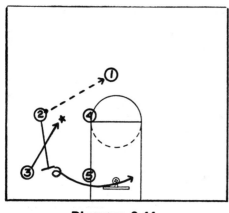

Diagram 2-14

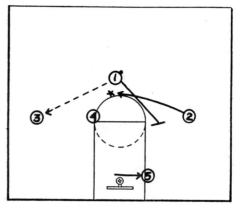

Diagram 2-15

BALANCING MOVES

To make the offense flow and give the movers more freedom, three balancing moves are added. They are the dribble chase, the quick cut, and the side "V" cut.

The Dribble Chase

At any time, but especially when the defense is overplaying and denying perimeter passes, the dribble chase is used. In Diagram 2-16, mover (1) cannot pass to (2) so he dribbles at him and clears him to the ball-side corner. This set would key the "Five Play" and its various options.

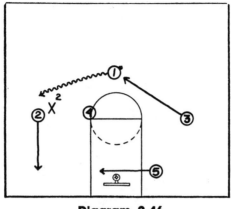

Diagram 2-16

The Quick Cut

The quick cut is a cut to the basket following a perimeter pass. It should be used when the defense is anticipating the pass and screen away. This time (Diagram 2-17), mover (1) passes to (2), steps toward (3), and then cuts off (4) for an easy basket.

The quick cut is also an excellent way to balance the offense from the "Five" set. In Diagram 2-18, (2) passes to point man (1), makes a quick cut, and moves to the offside wing. Mover (3) replaces (2) at the wing and the offense is balanced.

Note that (5) moved back to his original low-post position.

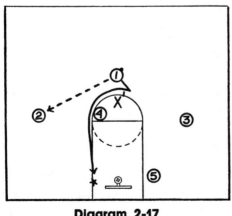

Diagram 2-17

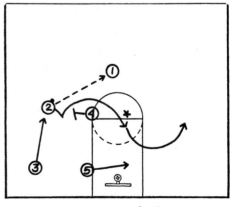

Diagram 2-18

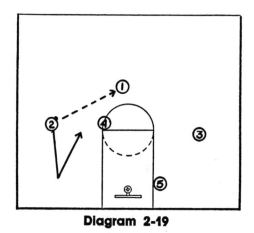

Diagram 2-19

The Side "V" Cut

The "V" cut is used when a side man passes to the point and has no one to screen away for. This cut helps keep the defense busy and allows (2) (in Diagram 2-19) to get open.

Post Play

The post men ((4) and (5)) should remember:

A. When you receive a pass, you should:
  - look for a shot.
  - expect the movers to split the post.
  - attempt to get the ball to the other post man.
  - know the third mover may be open.
B. You are the two primary rebounders.
C. To come to the ball-side on the "Five Play."
D. That the high-percentage play is to get the ball inside to the other post man.
E. That the two post men may change sides on an initial pass to a wing or a dribble entry.

RULES IN ACTION

Diagrams 2-20 through 2-30 show some play situations that may develop when the three-man passing game rules are utilized. Mover (1) passes and screens away (Diagram 2-20).

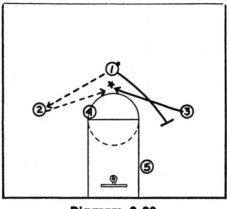

Diagram 2-20

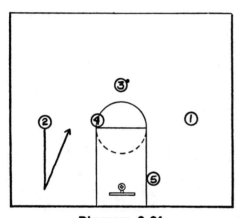

Diagram 2-21

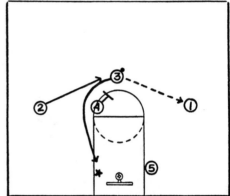

Diagram 2-22

After passing to (3), (2) makes a "V" cut (Diagram 2-21). Mover (3) passes and makes a quick cut off (4) for a possible lob pass from (1) (Diagram 2-22). Player (3) continues to the ball-side corner to set up a "Five Play" situation (Diagram 2-23). Player (1) cancels the "Five Play" with a quick cut (Diagram 2-24). Player (2) passes to (1) and screens away for (3). Player (3) does not use screen and (2) pops back to the point (Diagram 2-25). From this "Five Play" set, (1) passes to (2) and screens away for (3); (1) then clears to the offside (Diagram 2-26). Post man (5) breaks up, (2) passes to him and screens for (3). Player (1) is now third mover and cuts backdoor (Diagram 2-2⁷). Player (5) returns the ball to the perimeter by way of (3) (Diagram 2-28). Player (3) passes to (2) and loops around low-post man (4).

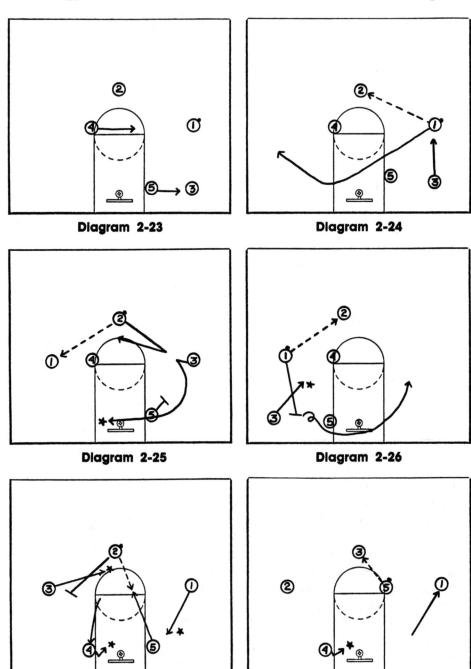

Diagram 2-23

Diagram 2-24

Diagram 2-25

Diagram 2-26

Diagram 2-27

Diagram 2-28

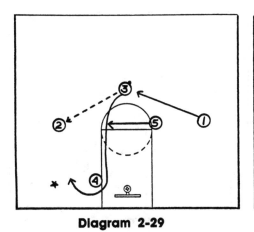

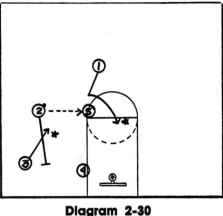

Diagram 2-29   **Diagram 2-30**

Player (1) takes the point. The "Five Play" set is formed (Diagram 2-29). Player (2) passes to (5) coming his way and screens for (3) in the corner. This play tells (1) to cut to the basket; (5) now feeds (4) inside for a score (Diagram 2-30).

The man-to-man phase of this offense forces the three small perimeter men to move and keeps the big men inside. The three simple rules provide a multiplicity of play situations that develop in a spontaneous and unpredictable fashion.

THE THREE-MAN PASSING GAME VERSUS ZONES

Many of the fundamentals of zone offense may be accomplished by way of the three-man passing game rules.

Overshift the Zone

In Diagram 2-31, point man (1) passes to wing man (2) and quick cuts down the lane and around the low-post man (5). The offside wing man (3) replaces (1) at the point and receives a pass from (2). He then reverses the ball to (1). Player (5) attempts to screen the zone and prevent the player in that area from covering (1). See Diagram 2-32.

This play is also an example of screening the overshift.

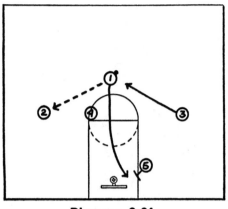
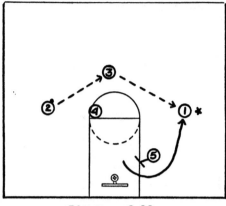

Diagram 2-31   **Diagram 2-32**

Overload the Zone

In Diagram 2-33, player (1) uses a dribble chase on wing man (2) and clears him to the corner. Mover (3) replaces (1) at the point. This "Five Play" set is, in effect, an overload.

When he wishes to, player (1) may cancel the overload by passing to (3) at the point and making a quick cut to the offside and be replaced by (2). See Diagrams 2-34 and 2-35.

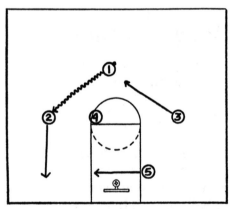
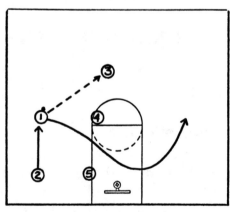

Diagram 2-33   **Diagram 2-34**

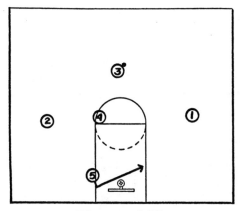

Diagram 2-35

Throw Post-to-Post Passes

One of the most difficult plays for a zone defense to handle is a perimeter pass to the high-post man ((4)), followed by a pass inside to the low-post man ((5)). The rules of this offense encourage the maneuver. See Diagram 2-36.

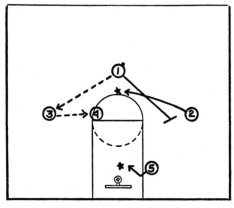

Diagram 2-36

CHANGING THE OFFENSIVE PERIMETER

The constant movement of the three movers offers many changes to the offensive perimeter. This is an especially difficult problem for adjusting zone defenses that key the offensive perimeter.

Check the Corner

The "Five Play" not only overloads the zone, but it forces corner coverage. The author feels the two moments of truth when playing zone defense are when the ball goes to the high post and when the defense must elongate and cover the corner.

Screen the Overload

Screening the overload may be accomplished by having point man (1) pass to the wing man on the low-post side and then cutting to that corner. Post man (5) then attempts to screen the zone and disallow coverage of the overloaded corner. See Diagrams 2-37 and 2-38.

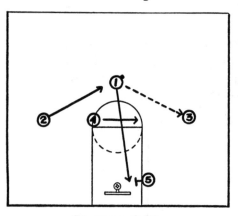

Diagram 2-37

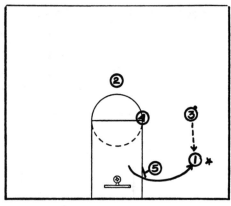

Diagram 2-38

The Second Side

The Three-Man Passing Game offense is a disciplined game and encourages many passes. The result is usually passes to both wings before a shot is taken, forcing the zone to work hard covering both sides of the court. Usually, the zone plan, including basic slides and personnel adjustments, becomes apparent.

Cover Defensive Balance

The point man in this offense is expected to be the first back on defense.

Have a Rebound Plan

Big men (4) and (5) are the primary rebounders and have no primary responsibilities in regard to defensive balance.

And finally, the unpredictability of this offense makes it difficult for zone teams to make their plans against it. The perimeter cuts are spontaneous and thoroughly test the mental discipline of the zone defenders.

Winning
Zone Offense

three

In my *Complete Book of Zone Game Basketball,* I mentioned that any zone offensive plan must consider the fundamentals of zone offense. They are:

1. Zones are vulnerable to the fast break.
2. Play your offensive-zone players between the zone defenders and "split" the zone.
3. Read the zone's intent and make your plans accordingly. Are the defenders putting pressure on the perimeter or are they packing the lane?
4. Have a plan that makes the zone come out and then get the ball inside.
5. Have a rebound plan. Zone teams want to give you one hurried outside shot.
6. Expect to shoot from the outside. Take a good look at your offense. Know where the outside shots will be taken and spot shoot in practice.
7. Move the ball at a planned tempo. "Hot potato" does not work. Teach your players to fake and then pass.
8. Throw crosscourt passes. Zone teams seldom practice against them.

9. Send cutters through. It forces the zone to tighten up and results in better outside shots.

10. Vary the offensive perimeter. Matching zones key on the opposition's offensive front, in regard to whether it is odd or even.

11. Overload the zone. Make the zone work hard.

12. Overshift the zone by quickly reversing the ball to the other side.

13. Screen the overshift. Screens work well against zones.

14. Test the corner.

15. Test the middle.

16. Go second side. Never shoot any shot but a lay-up or wide-open shot on the first penetration.

17. Take advantage of your personnel match-ups. Man-to-man defenses determine the match-ups, but in the zone game, the offense makes this determination.

18. Run your man-to-man offense as a secondary zone attack. When things are not going well, give them something different to look at. Then come back to your zone offense.

19. Use the dribble to penetrate and/or rotate the zone defense's perimeter.

20. Teach the players to receive the ball in an all-purpose position.

21. Put a big man out front and throw over the small front-zone defenders.

22. Teach players to slide into the weak areas of the zone.

23. Pass post-to-post. Hit the high-post man and then have him pass to the low-post man. Pass to the low post and have him look for the high-post man cutting down toward the basket.

24. Have a pressure defense ready. Change the tempo when things are not going well.

25. Overcome the fear of zones. Include zone offense in every practice plan.

The following seven zone offensive series utilize the fundamentals of zone offense, within the context of functional movement. I chose to refer to them as series rather than offenses because many of their components are interchangeable. A coach should decide which of the various maneuvers fit his personnel and put together a tailor-made zone offensive plan. Many of these series feature the triangle play which I feel is the best zone play. It offers a method of getting the ball inside against the zone. Also included is a section on dribble-entry play against zone defenses.

SERIES I—A BASIC FOUR-MAN MOTION

This series is designed for a team with one big post man and four players who can shoot from the perimeter. The four outside players must be able to play either guard or forward.

The play begins (as shown in Diagram 3-1) with guard (1) passing to forward (3). The offside guard (2) then cuts to the ball-side corner to form an overload in conjunction with players (1), (3), and post man (5), who has swung to the ball-side.

The team then searches for an open shot as they utilize the passing triangles formed by the overload. Player (4) becomes the primary offside rebounder. See Diagram 3-2.

When it is desirable to change the overload, the change is keyed by wing man (3). This change may be done in one of two

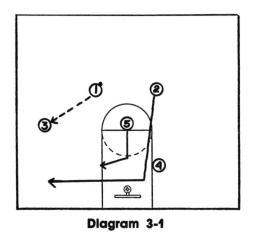

Diagram 3-1

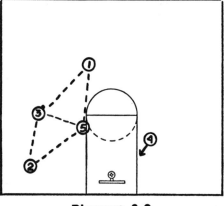

Diagram 3-2

38

ways: Player (3) may pass to (2) in the corner and cut through, or player (3) may pass to point man (1) and cut through.

Pass to Corner

Forward (3) passes to corner man (2) and cuts through to the weakside, the offensive perimeter rotates toward the ball with (1) replacing (3) at the wing, (4) replacing (1) at the point, and (3) becoming the offside wing man (Diagram 3-3). The ball is then reversed to (3). Note that the post man (5) and corner man (2) also move to the ball-side. See Diagrams 3-4 and 3-5.

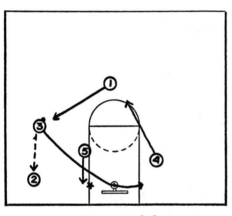

Diagram 3-3

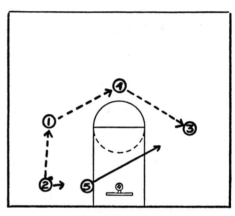

Diagram 3-4

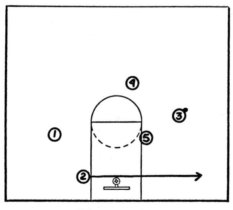

Diagram 3-5

Pass to Point

Player (3) can also change the overload by (using the positions in Diagram 3-5 above) passing to point man (4) and cutting through to the far side. When this occurs, the team returns to a two-man front with (4) moving to the ball-side to receive (3)'s pass, (1) becoming the second guard and (2) moving up to replace (3). See Diagrams 3-6 and 3-7. The team may now stay in a two-man front or cut a guard through to the ball-side corner and return to a one-man front. This ability to change the perimeter of your zone offense is very effective versus adjusting zones. Anytime the team is in a one-man front, the point man ((4) in Diagram 3-8) can use another method to return the offense to a two-man front. He does this by dribbling away from the overloaded side. This key tells the corner man (2) to dip toward the basket and then move out front, off a downscreen by the onside wing man (3). See Diagram 3-9.

From there, the series may be restarted.

The four perimeter players must do a lot of practice shooting from the wings, the point, and the corner. The post man must move in a triangle motion and search for opportunities for an inside power jump shot.

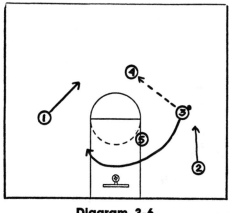

Diagram 3-6

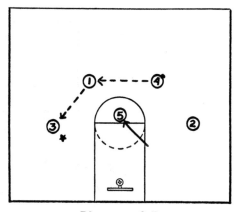

Diagram 3-7

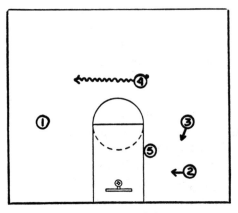

Diagram 3-8

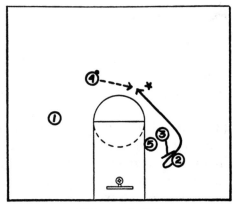

Diagram 3-9

SERIES II—A FOUR-MAN CONTINUITY SERIES

This series is for a team with no big men or four players ((2), (3), (4), and (5) in Diagram 3-10) with the same abilities inside and on the perimeter. It may be run as a zone offense and as a man-to-man alternative. Player (1) is the point man, feeder, and usually the first man back on defense.

The series is initiated as point man (1) passes to wing man (as to (2) in Diagram 3-11). This tells the offside post man (5) to cut to the high-post area. If (2) can pass to him, (5) may shoot,

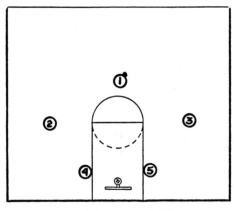

Diagram 3-10

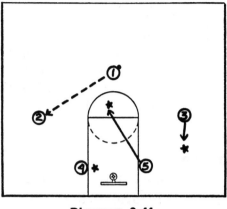

Diagram 3-11

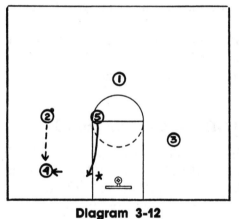

Diagram 3-12

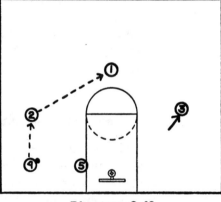

Diagram 3-13

look for (4) inside the zone, or reverse it to (3) in the offside wing area.

If (2) cannot get the ball to (5), (4) breaks to the ball-side corner, and receives a pass from him. This pass tells (5) to slide to a low-post position while looking for a pass from (4). See Diagram 3-12.

If player (4) cannot shoot or get the ball to (5) inside, he reverses it to (1) at the point by way of (2). Note that (3) then moved to the offside wing area. See Diagram 3-13.

From there, either of two plays may occur: the offside screen, or the downscreen.

The Offside Screen

Player (5) steps out and screens for (4) who cuts above him and to the offside-post area. Actually, this cut is a better man-to-man maneuver, but it may provide a shot if (5) traps the zone in the corner. It is more likely, however, that (5) will be open after (4)'s cut for a lob pass inside the zone by (1). See Diagram 3-14 and 3-15.

The Downscreen

After (4) has cut, and point man (1) has looked for (5) inside the zone, (1) fakes to (3) as (2) downscreens for (5). Player (5) pops out to the wing as (2) attempts to trap the zone inside. This maneuver is also a strong man-to-man play. See Diagram 3-16.

As soon as player (1) passes to (5) (or to (3) if (5) is not open), the offside post man (4) in Diagram 3-17 cuts to the high-post area and the same series is run again.

SERIES III—THE FORWARD-CALL SERIES

The ball may be entered on either side in the Forward Call Series. This option makes the offside forward ((4) in Diagram 3-18) the player who will key the play. Players (1), (2), (3), and (4) are interchangeable and (5) is the big post man.

After player (1) passes to (3), he cuts to the offside wing in a looping motion. Post man (5) swings to the ball side, (2) moves to the point, and (4), the offside forward, may call one of three options. He does this by the direction of his cut. He may: Move out front to call "motion," cut to the offside corner to designate an overload, or cut to the middle to key the high-low play.

Motion

In Diagram 3-19, offside forward (4) chooses to move out front and is replaced by player (1). This motion changes the offense from a two-man front to a one-man front, when (1) cuts through, and back to a two-man front once (4) moves out front and (1) replaces him. See Diagram 3-19 and 3-20.

This movement may cause difficulty for an adjusting zone.

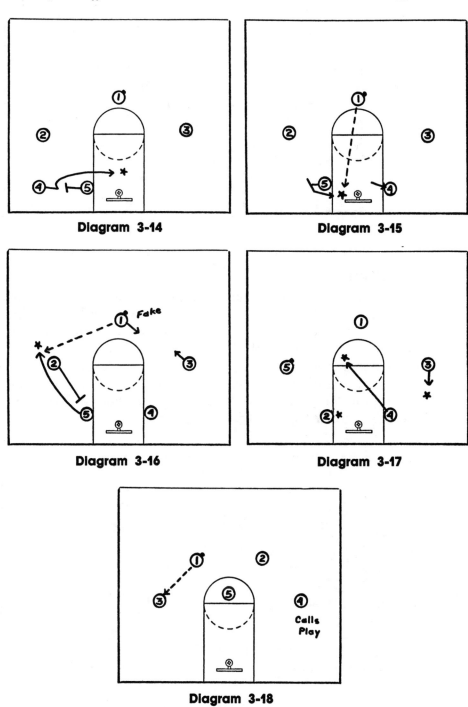

Diagram 3-14

Diagram 3-15

Diagram 3-16

Diagram 3-17

Diagram 3-18

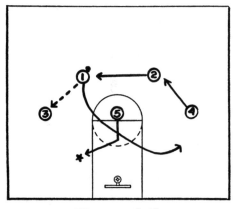

Diagram 3-19

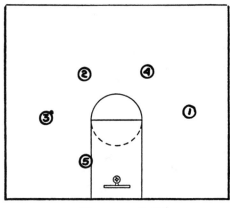

Diagram 3-20

Overload

This time, after (1) cuts through, (4) calls an overload by cutting to the ball-side corner. (Diagrams 3-21 and 3-22). The passing triangles formed by this overload are then utilized until the ball is reversed to (1). See Diagram 3-23.

When this reversal happens, player (4) swings to the ball-side corner and (1) may utilize the new overload on that side (Diagram 3-24); he may also decide to dribble out front to restart the offense. See Diagram 3-25.

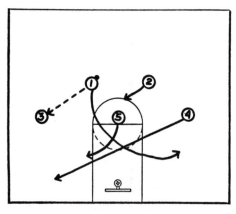

Diagram 3-21

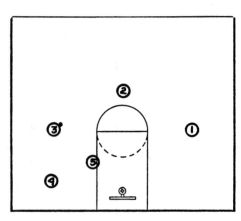

Diagram 3-22

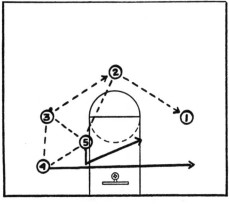

Diagram 3-23

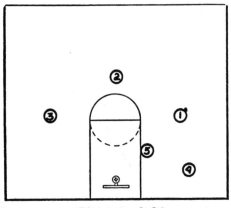

Diagram 3-24

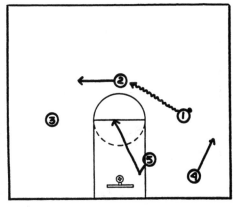

Diagram 3-25

The Middle Cut

Player (1) passes to (3) and cuts through the key, while (4) makes a middle cut. If (4) can receive a pass from (3), he may shoot, look for (5) inside the zone, or reverse it to (1) at the off-side wing. See Diagrams 3-26 and 3-27.

If player (3) cannot get the ball to (4), he passes to (2) and cuts to the offside wing area; player (1) then moves out front, and (4) takes (3)'s wing. See Diagrams 3-28 and 3-29.

The team is then in position to run either of three plays with the offside wing man again making the call.

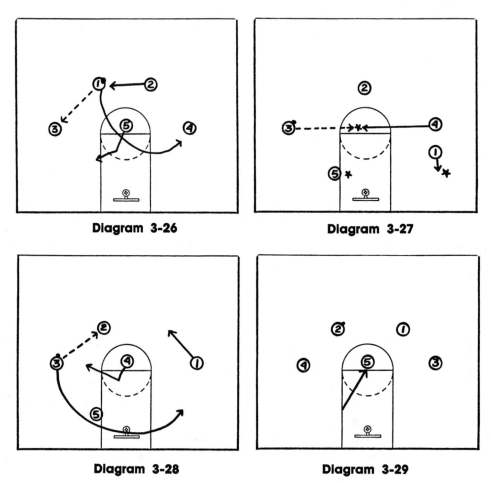

Diagram 3-26   Diagram 3-27

Diagram 3-28   Diagram 3-29

SERIES IV—THE DOUBLE-POST TRIANGLE SERIES

This offense is best used by a team with two big men ((4) and (5) in Diagram 3-30) and three movers, (1), (2), and (3). It begins when point man (1) passes to wing man (2). This pass tells the offside wing man (3) to cut to the high-post area.

Triangle Play

If (3) receives a pass from (2), he may shoot, or look inside the zone for big men (4) and (5). See Diagram 3-31.

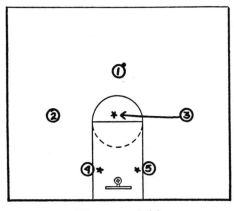

Diagram 3-30

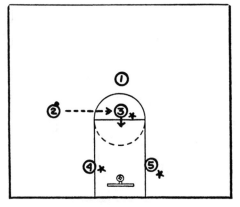

Diagram 3-31

Double Screen

If (2) cannot pass to mover (3), he passes back to (1) at the point and moves down to form a double screen with (4). Player (3) uses the double screen as he loops down around it and (2) and (4) attempt to trap the zone inside. See Diagram 3-32.

Mover (1) can help (3) get open near the double screen if he fakes a pass to (5), who has moved out toward the wing, and then passes back to (3) (Diagram 3-33). If (3) is not open, he passes back to (1), who reverses the ball to (2), looping around (5)'s downscreen. Big man (5) tries to trap the zone inside and prevent it from covering (2). See Diagram 3-34.

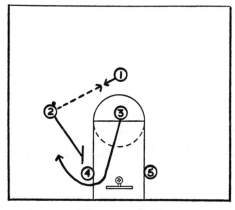

Diagram 3-32

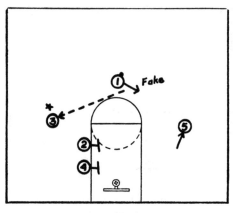

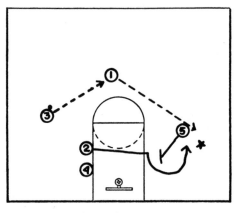

Diagram 3-33   **Diagram 3-34**

Restart

Once (2) receives the ball, mover (3) cuts to the middle and the series starts over. See Diagram 3-35.

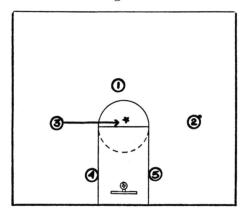

Diagram 3-35

SERIES V—A TRIANGLE SERIES FEATURING A 1-3-1 SET WITH A BASELINE ROAMER

Series V is an offense for a team with one big man to play the post, (5). Player (1) is always the point man and is expected to be the first man back on defense. Players (2) and (3) are the

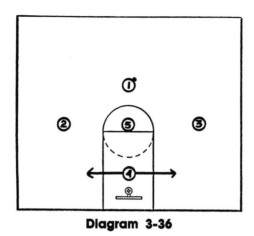

Diagram 3-36

wing men and should be good jump shooters from that area. Player (4) is the baseline roamer. See Diagram 3-36.

Triangle Cut

The play begins as (1) passes to a wing man ((2) in Diagram 3-37) and cuts away. This pass and cut tells (4) to post up on that side and (5) to play the offside post. The offside wing man ((3)) then cuts to the middle for a possible triangle play. See Diagram 3-38.

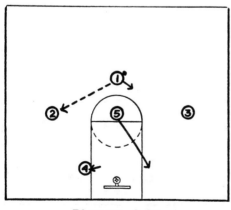

Diagram 3-37

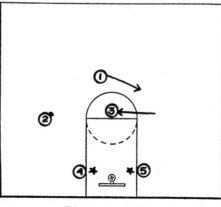

Diagram 3-38

Corner Play

If (2) cannot pass to (3), baseline roamer (4) cuts to the ball-side corner and receives a pass from (2) (Diagram 3-39). Note that at times, (2) can throw a crosscourt pass to (1) for a jump shot; (2) then cuts through and acts as a natural screen as (5) cuts to the ball-side low-post area. See Diagram 3-40.

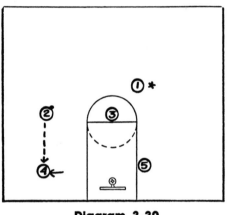

Diagram 3-39

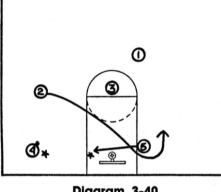

Diagram 3-40

Reverse and Restart

If player (4) is unable to get the ball to (5), (3) pops out to the ball-side wing, and (4) reverses the ball to (3), who can reverse to (1) and to (2). At the same time, (4) cuts off (5) to the ballside. See Diagrams 3-41 and 3-42.

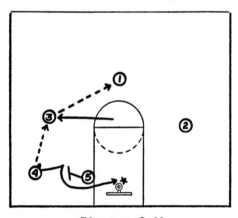

Diagram 3-41

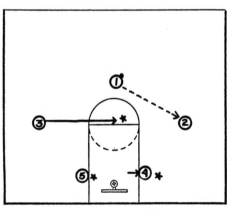

Diagram 3-42

This resets the offense and the same sequence is repeated.

A very similar pattern may be used when (4) and (5) are both big men.

SERIES VI—THE POST-TO-WING TRIANGLE SERIES

Point man (1) passes to (2), and (3) cuts to the middle for the triangle option. If (3) is not open, he continues to the ball-side corner. See Diagram 3-43.

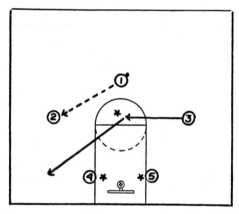

Diagram 3-43

Reverse It

Player (2) utilizes the overload and then passes to (1), who reverses the ball to post man (5), who has moved out to the wing position (Diagrams 3-44 and 3-45). Player (2) then cuts to the ball-side corner, (4) swings over to the ball-side post, and (3) moves up to replace (2) (Diagram 3-46). This activity switches the overload to (5)'s side of the court.

Players (1), (2), (4), and (5) then utilize the passing triangles of the overload. Once the ball is reversed by (1) to (3), (5) cuts back to the ball-side-post area. See Diagrams 3-47 and 3-48.

The players are then back in their basic positions ((1) at the point, (2) and (3) at the wings, and (4) and (5) in the posts). From there, a new sequence can be initiated by a wing man (as shown by (3) in Diagram 3-49) cutting to the middle.

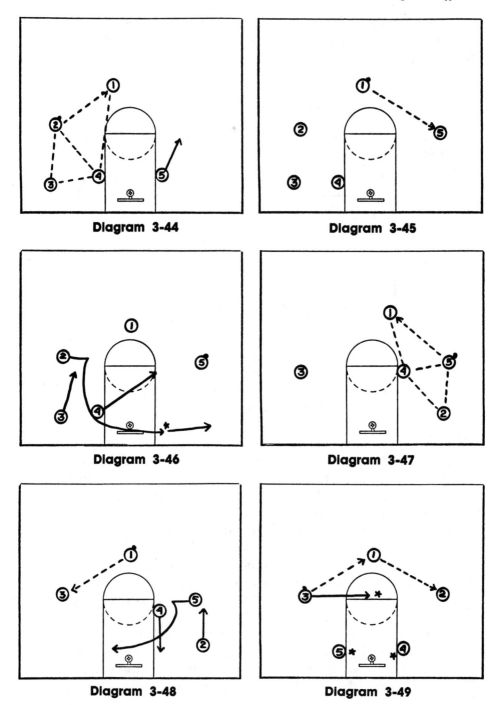

Diagram 3-44

Diagram 3-45

Diagram 3-46

Diagram 3-47

Diagram 3-48

Diagram 3-49

SERIES VII—THE "T-GAME" ZONE SERIES

Dribble Entry

This series features two big men, (4) and (5); two guards, (1) and (2); and a corner man with the attributes of a strong forward, (3). The series begins as guard (1) (in Diagram 3-50) dribbles to the wing area on his side. This dribble tells (3) to cut to the ball-side corner, post man (5) to move to the low-post area, and (4) to cross with (5) on his cut to the high post. This maneuver is also an excellent man-to-man move because it takes away the offside help on the low post.

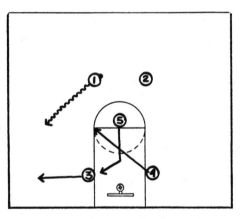

Diagram 3-50

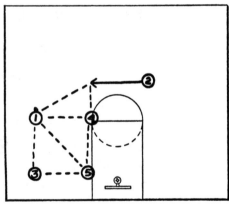

Diagram 3-51

Player (1)'s first option is to look inside to one of the post players ((4) in the high post or (5) in the low post). If neither is open for a shot, the team can utilize the overload triangles. See Diagram 3-51.

If (1) decides to switch the overload, he passes to player (3) in the corner, cuts through for a possible return pass from (3), and then loops to the offside-guard area; (2) moves to the ball-side-guard area. See Diagram 3-52.

Player (3) passes to (2), who passes to (1). Player (3) then cuts off (5) to (1)'s side of the court. See Diagram 3-53.

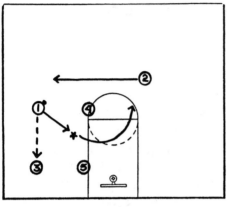

Diagram 3-52

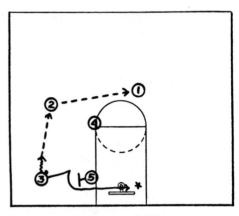

Diagram 3-53

Restart

Player (3)'s cut is an excellent man-to-man option; (1) then makes a dribble entry to the wing area to initiate a new sequence. See Diagram 3-54.

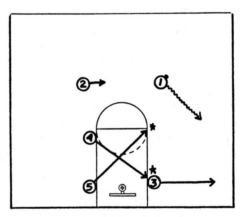

Diagram 3-54

OTHER DRIBBLE-ENTRY PLAYS

The following dribble-entry plays may be added to any of the seven series. These plays will force defensive adjustments by varying the offensive perimeter, putting a big man out front, and by using the dribble entry to form an overload. In some cases, the dribble-entry series can be used to initiate another series. This last attribute is demonstrated as it is used to initiate Series III. These examples are only a few of how this maneuver may be utilized against zone defenses.

Varying the Offensive Perimeter

In Diagram 3-55, guard (1) dribbles at forward (3) and clears him to the offside-forward position. Guard (1) then stops and passes back to (2), who reverses the ball to (3) coming around (4)'s downscreen.

This quick reversal is a strong scoring option and converts the offense from a 2-1-2 to a 1-2-2 set.

In Diagram 3-56, a similar play is run to convert the 1-2-2 offense to a 2-3 set. Point man (1) dribbles toward (2)'s sideline.

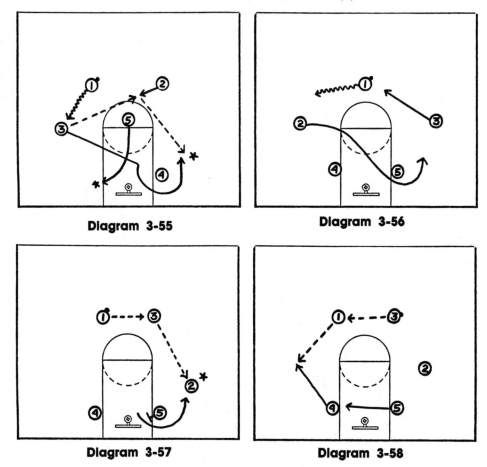

Diagram 3-55

Diagram 3-56

Diagram 3-57

Diagram 3-58

This movement clears wing man (2) down and around the offside post man (5). Offside wing man (3) moves out front. The ball is then reversed back to (2) by way of (3). See Diagram 3-57.

If player (2) is not open and the ball comes back to (4)'s side, he breaks up-court, and the team is then in a 2-3 set. See Diagram 3-58.

Putting a Big Man Out Front

In Diagram 3-59, (1) dribbles at (3) and clears him down and around post man (5). At the same time, the offside guard loops down and around the forward on his side. This move converts the 2-1-2 offense to a 1-2-2 set, puts a tall man ((3)) out front who can see over the small front defenders and places a good shooter on each wing ((1) and (2)). See Diagram 3-60.

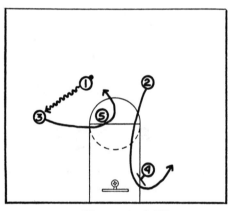

Diagram 3-59

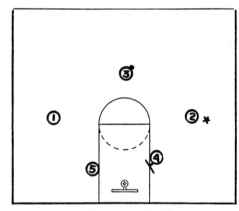

Diagram 3-60

Using the Dribble Entry to Form an Overload

This play provides two methods of creating an overload. Player (3) is the key man; when (1) dribbles at him, he may: clear to the corner, or loop out front.

Player (3) Clears to the Corner

In Diagram 3-61, (1) dribbles at (3) and he ((3)) clears to the corner. Player (2) may then become the single point man by cutting directly to the ball side or looping around (5) and to the ball-side point. This movement creates an overload. See Diagram 3-62.

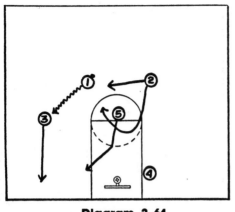

Diagram 3-61

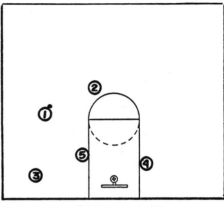

Diagram 3-62

Player (3) Loops Out Front

In Diagram 3-63, player (1) dribbles at (3) and (3) loops around (5) to the ball-side point position. Player (3)'s cut tells (2) to cut to the ball-side corner. This play also creates an overload. See Diagram 3-64.

An entire series may be run with a dribble entry if desired. Diagrams 3-65 and 3-66 show *The Forward Call Series* being run with (1) making the dribble entry and the offside forward (4) calling the "motion" play.

Diagrams 3-67 and 3-68 show (1) making the dribble entry and the offside forward (4) calling the Middle Cut Play.

Diagrams 3-69 and 3-70 show player (1) making the dribble entry and (4) calling the overload by cutting to the ball-side corner.

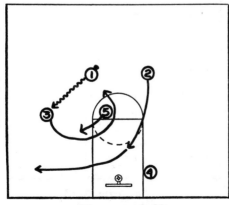

Diagram 3-63

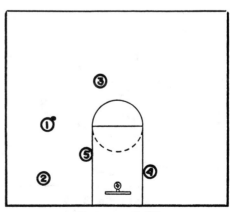

Diagram 3-64

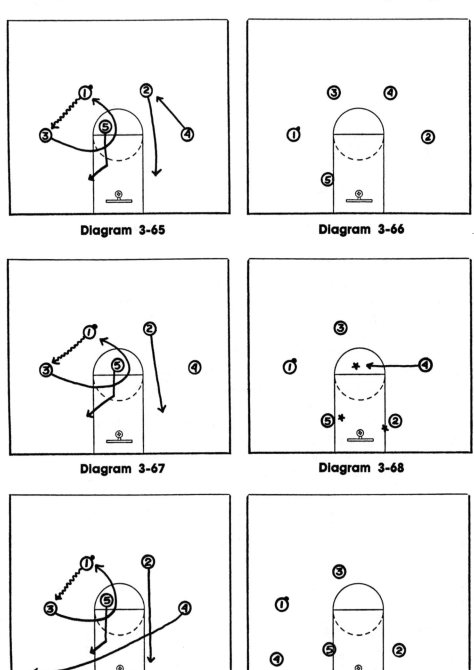

Diagram 3-65

Diagram 3-66

Diagram 3-67

Diagram 3-68

Diagram 3-69

Diagram 3-70

Note that players (1), (2), (3), and (5) make the same cuts on all three options. The same reset maneuvers may be utilized when desired.

The wide variety of offensive sets, personnel requirements, and play situations presented in these seven zone series allow a coach to choose those that best fit his situation. The plays are motion-oriented and utilize the fundamentals of zone offense to present viable zone offensive plans. The dribble entry may be used to provide variety.

An Offensive Full-Court Traffic Pattern

|| four

The following full-court traffic pattern is more than a fast-break plan. It is a pattern that may be run: When the opposition fails to score and you want to attempt to fast break from a missed field goal; when the opposition fails to score and you want to fast break from a missed free throw; when the opposition scores and you want to run the ball up-court in an organized fashion; when the opposition scores and applies a full-court zone press, and finally, when the opposition scores and applies man-to-man pressure.

FAST BREAK FROM A MISSED FIELD GOAL

In Diagram 4-1, the opposition missed a field goal and our player (4) obtained the rebound. The front man on his side, (2), wings out to take the outlet pass. We want (4) to pivot to the outside, and the outlet man (2) to receive the ball with his shoulders parallel to the sideline, permitting him to see the entire court upon receiving the ball. The offside front man, (1), cuts diagonally to the ball-side midcourt line while looking for a pass from (2). Player (5), who is the offensive pivot man and defensive safety man, moves up-court slowly. Players (4) and (3) attempt to fill the outside lanes on their respective sides of the

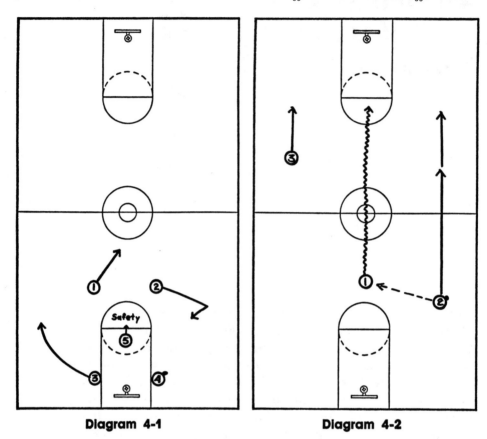

Diagram 4-1   **Diagram 4-2**

court. From there three plays may occur. The plays are: the Pass to Middle, the Dribble to Middle, and the Hook Back.

Pass to Middle

If outlet man (2) can pass to (1) in the middle, (2) fills the outside lane and (1) takes the ball up the middle. See Diagram 4-2.

Trailer Play

Player (1) stops at the free throw line and players (2) and (3) make their diagonal cuts to the blocks. See Diagram 4-3.

If (2) and (3) are not open, (3) screens down, and the outlet-side wing man (2) runs through; this cut through by (2)

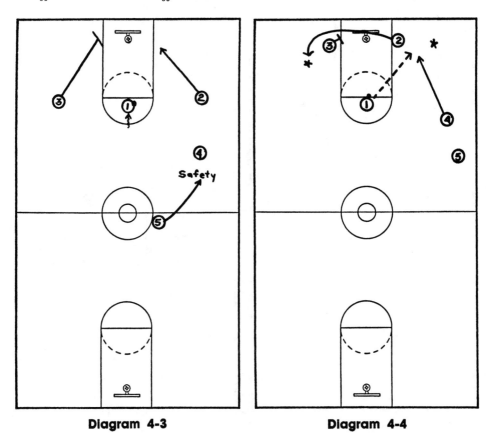

Diagram 4-3   **Diagram 4-4**

provides a trailer lane for (4) who gets the pass from (1) for a lay-up shot (Diagram 4-4). Note that the rebounder is the trailer.

Early Offense

If early offense is desired, player (2) can loop around (3) and receive a pass from (1). Player (4), after cutting to the basket, wings out and screens for trailer (5) coming down the sideline. Player (2) may shoot, lob to (5), or look for (3) inside. See Diagram 4-5.

If no one is open, player (2) dribbles out front and the team is in position to run the basic offense. See Diagram 4-6.

This early-offense option may be run with any of the fast-break options.

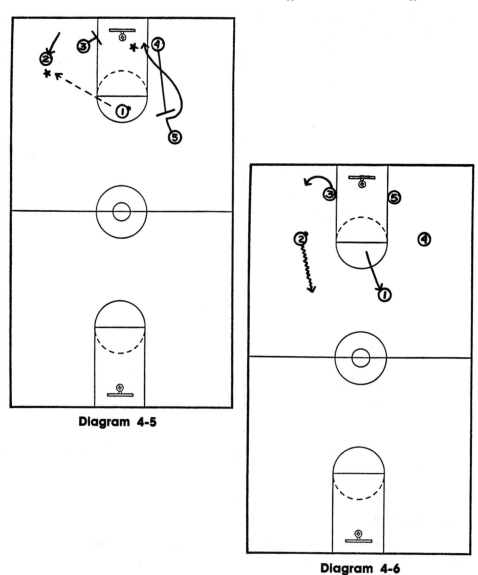

Diagram 4-5

Diagram 4-6

Dribble to Middle

This time, player (2) cannot get the ball to (1) in the middle. Player (1) continues his diagonal cut to the ball-side and (2) dribbles to the middle. Rebounder (4) becomes the trailer in the outlet lane and (5) is the safety man. See Diagrams 4-7 and 4-8.

The same trailer and early offense options may be run.

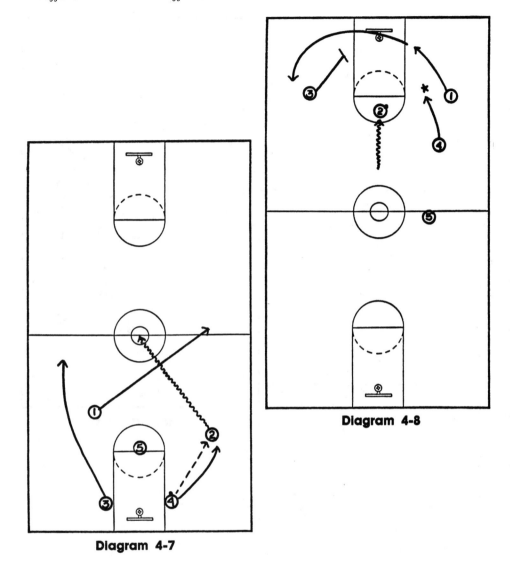

Diagram 4-8

Diagram 4-7

Hook Back

This time the opposition plays for the outlet pass by fronting (2). Player (1) makes his diagonal cut, player (2) moves back to the middle, and (4), unable to pass to (2), dribbles to the outside and upcourt. See Diagram 4-9.

Player (4) then passes to (1) hooking back; (1) takes the ball to the middle and players (2) and (4) race for the ball-side out-

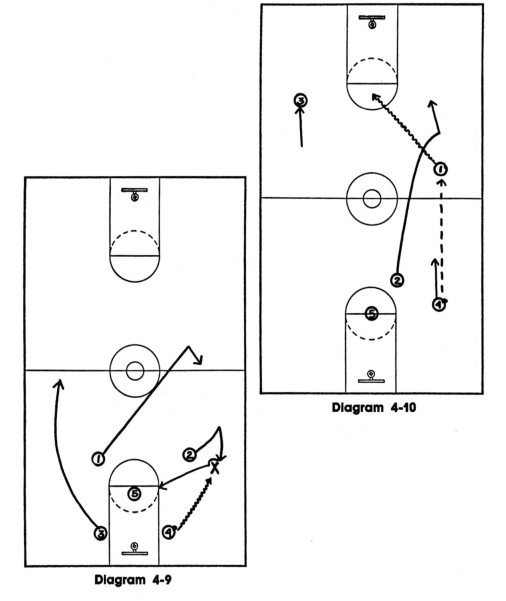

Diagram 4-10

Diagram 4-9

side lane. The first one there fills the lane and runs through it and the second becomes the trailer. Player (5) is the safety man. See Diagrams 4-10 and 4-11.

The same early offense options may be run.

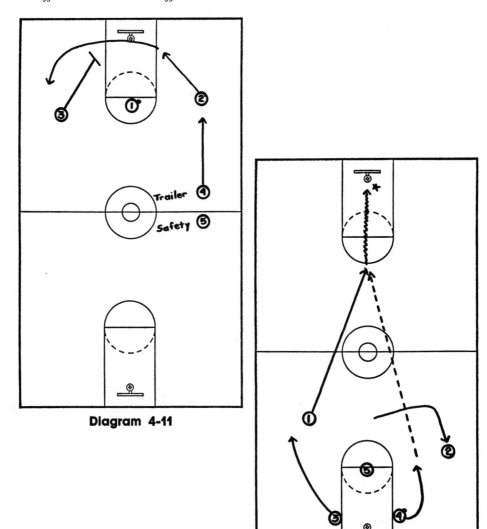

Diagram 4-11

Diagram 4-12

Last-Second-Shot Option

When the opposition delays for the last shot and it is taken, the offside front man ((1) in Diagram 4-12) takes off for the basket and the outlet passer ((4)) may throw a desperation pass.

FAST BREAK FROM A MISSED FREE THROW

In Diagram 4-13, the opposition is shooting a free throw. The two biggest men, (4) and (5), line up inside. Player (3) cuts off the shooter and then fills the lane on the side opposite (4). Big man (5) is the safety man.

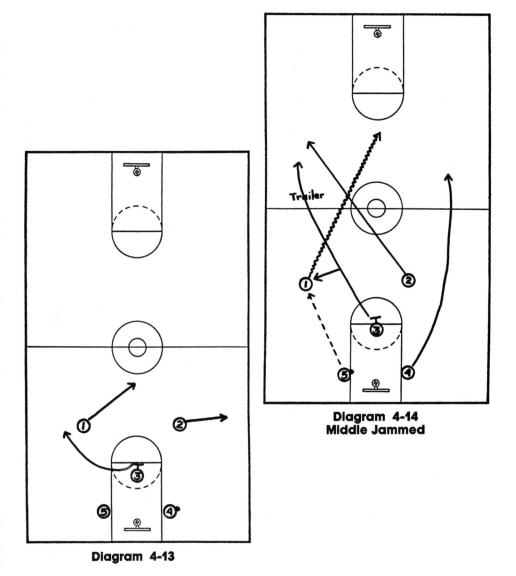

Diagram 4-14
Middle Jammed

Diagram 4-13

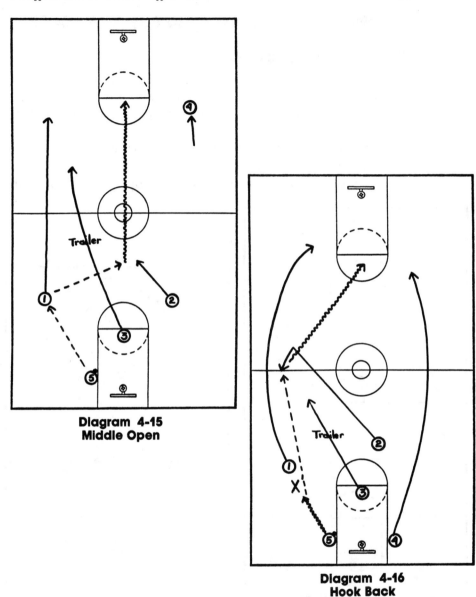

Diagram 4-15
Middle Open

Diagram 4-16
Hook Back

The pattern's options are the same as after a missed field goal. Player (5) is always the safety man. When he rebounds, (3) still fills that lane. See Diagrams 4-14, 4-15, and 4-16. Note in these three options that (3) is the trailer when (5) rebounds.

RUNNING THE BALL UP-COURT AFTER A SCORE

The Opposition Scores

Player (5) takes the ball out of the net, jumps out-of-bounds, and passes to (2). Player (1) makes his diagonal cut and (3) and (4) sprint up-court in their respective lanes. See Diagram 4-17.

In Diagram 4-18, player (2) dribbles to the middle and that pattern is run quickly up-court.

The same trailer and early offense options may be run.

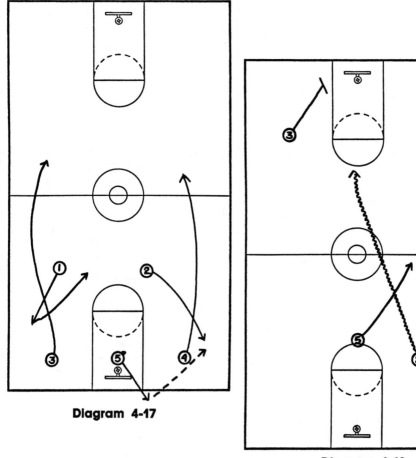

Diagram 4-17

Diagram 4-18

The Opposition Scores and Applies a Full-Court Press

The full-court traffic pattern may also be run after the opposition scores and sets up a full-court zone press. In Diagram 4-19, the team has run their initial cuts with (5) taking the ball out, (2) coming toward the ball to receive the inbounds pass, players (3) and (4) streaking downcourt in their respective outside lanes and (1) coming to the ball and, after seeing the pass made to (2), cutting diagonally across the middle.

This time, however, (2) is double-teamed upon receiving the ball and the opposition shows zone press by its defensive formation. Player (2) then has these options:

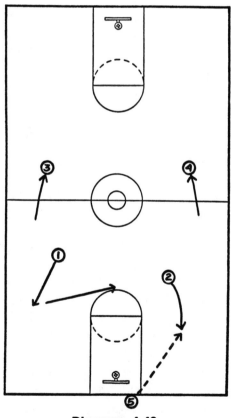

Diagram 4-19

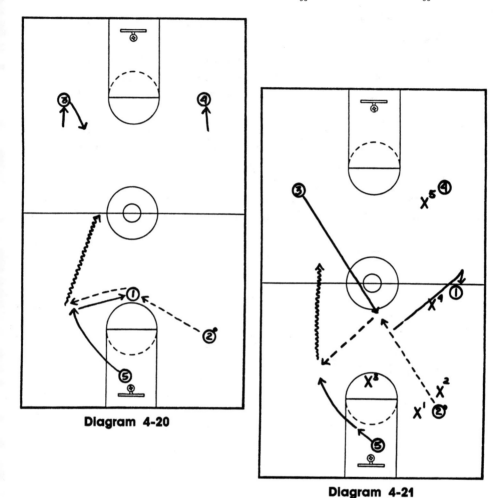

Diagram 4-20

Diagram 4-21

A. If (2) can quickly get the ball to (1), (1) must catch it as he makes a jump stop in a spread-out-wide stance. When this happens, (1) reverses the ball to (5) going up the open sideline. See Diagram 4-20. We suggest that (2)'s pass to (1) be a two-hand overhead pass.

B. If (2) cannot get the ball to player (1), (1) continues his cut to the ball-side sideline and the offside downcourt man (3) cuts to the middle. Player (4) moves downcourt. This pass would also be reversed to (5) on the open sideline. See Diagram 4-21.

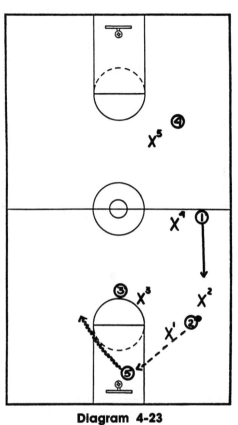

Diagram 4-23

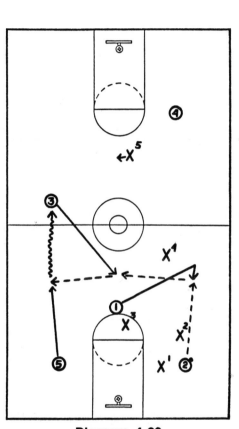

Diagram 4-22

C. Player (2) may pass to (1) at the sideline. When he passes, (3) cuts to the ball, and if he receives it, (3) reverses it to (5). See Diagram 4-22.

D. Player (2) may also pass the ball to (5) behind the double-team. When this pass occurs, (5) dribbles toward the open side and (1) and (3) change assignments with (1) cutting to the middle and (3) moving to the ball-side sideline (Diagrams 4-23 and 4-24). Player (5) then has the same options previously open to (2). Ideally, he pas-

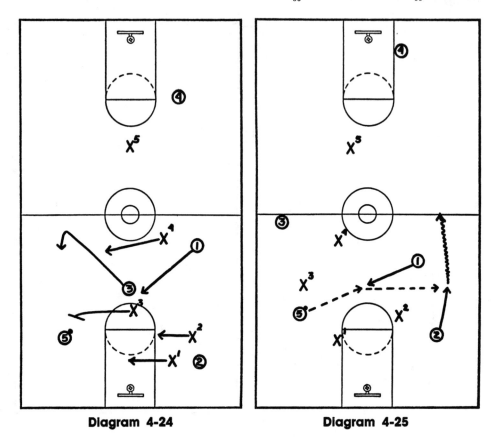

Diagram 4-24   **Diagram 4-25**

ses to (1), who reverses the ball to (2), who brings the ball up the open sideline. See Diagram 4-25.

It must be pointed out that (5) must be an above-average ball handler. If your big man is not very agile, you may change his assignments with the most agile forward.

The Opposition Scores and Picks Up Man-to-Man

One of the techniques we teach our guards to use when bringing the ball up-court is "the loop." We use a 2-2 full court drill that teaches the offensive guard without the ball to give the

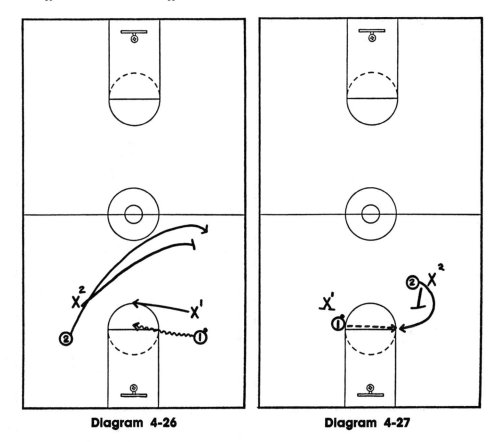

Diagram 4-26   **Diagram 4-27**

guard with the ball the entire floor by making a looping cut. Diagram 4-26 shows the drill with guard (2) clearing out and permitting (1) to dribble to any portion of the court without fear of being double-teamed.

If (1) is forced to pick up his dribble, player (2) must return to a position as high as the ball and get open for a pass from (1). See Diagram 4-27.

The same process is then repeated with (1) making the loop. We expect our guards to be able to bring the ball up-court against man-to-man pressure.

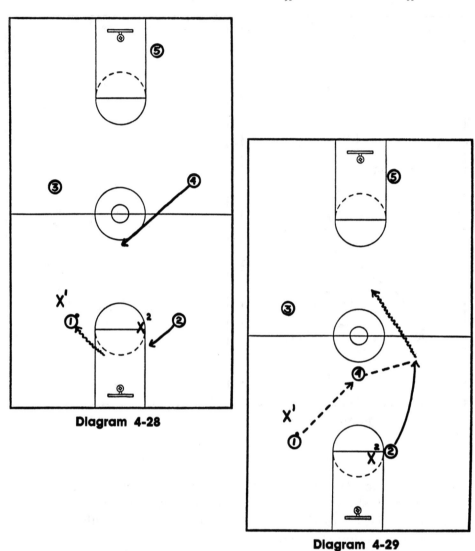

Diagram 4-28

Diagram 4-29

The loop is used within the context of the pattern versus man-to-man pressure. To aid the guards, (5) must be careful to keep his defender away from the dribbler and cut to the ball when a guard gets in trouble. The two downcourt men, (3) and (4), watch the ball and cut to the middle from the offside when a guard picks up his dribble. See (4) in Diagram 4-28.

If a pass is then made to (4) cutting into the middle, he ((4)) looks to reverse it to (2) and the result is very much like a backdoor play against a man-to-man defense. See Diagram 4-29.

Having an all-purpose pattern of this sort saves a lot of practice time. However, the coach must be sure to point out the subtle differences that permit the pattern to be run in the various situations. A good job of scouting can make the players more aware of what to expect from the opposition and how to react in the context of the pattern.

Defeating the Zone Press

five

The following zone-pressure offensive patterns are innovative methods of counteracting the plans of zone-pressure defenses. These offensive patterns are predicated on the fact that the "Achilles Heel" of the zone press is its middle, and are designed to take advantage of this fact. The various patterns include: *The Trailing Big Man Pattern* that offers a new approach to defeating zone presses; *A Moving Pattern* that makes it difficult for the defense to anticipate your plan; *A Second Moving Pattern* with a novel twist; and *A Multipurpose Plan* that may be used as a full-court press pattern, a half-court pattern, or as a device to stall and force standard zone defenses to come out and cover one-half of the court area.

THE TRAILING-BIG-MAN ZONE-PRESS OFFENSE

The Trailing-Big-Man zone-press offense is designed to take advantage of the inherent weaknesses of the zone-press defense. Most of these defenses attempt to double-team the inbounds pass and deny the pass to the middle. At the same time, they must protect against the long pass. Because they are so conscious of these goals, they are very vulnerable to a reversal of the ball to the opposite side. Teams have always tried to do this by passing forward into the middle of the press and then to the weak side. This is a very functional, but risky, technique. This offense has an alternate method of reversing the ball. It is done by way of a backward pass to a trailing big man.

Inbounding the Ball

The ball is taken out by the agile big man ((3) in Diagram 5-1). The fact that (3) is tall is an advantage in itself since he can see over the press, and it also allows for two agile inbounds pass receivers (guards (1) and (2)). If the opposition is denying the inbounds pass, the guards may cross before attempting to receive it. If possible, the pass should be received just inside the free throw line extended. The receivers should be moving to-

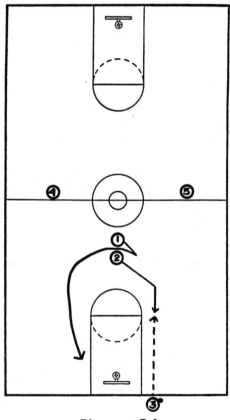

Diagram 5-1

ward the passer to minimize interceptions. The fact that the inbounds pass is received this far downcourt permits players (4)
and (5) to also play further downcourt, and this elongates the
zone press.

Pass to the Middle

Once the ball is inbounded (as to (2) in Diagram 5-2), the
offside downcourt man (4) breaks to the middle. If this pass can
be completed, the ball is then reversed to (1) and taken down
the weak side. (Note: We teach (2) to use a two-hand overhead
pass when he is double-teamed.) The problem with this method
is that most zone-pressure teams expect this pass and work very
hard to prevent it. Diagram 5-3 shows a typical zone press and
how X3 will deny the pass to (4).

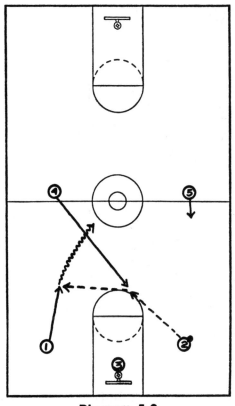

Diagram 5-2

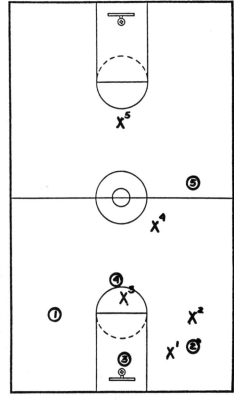

Diagram 5-3

Dangerous Reversal

In the past, when teams did not use the trailing big man concept and could not get the ball in the middle, they still attempted to reverse the ball, but they did it with a flat pass parallel to the free throw line (guard-to-guard pass). The pass across the free throw line was very dangerous and led to many baskets by the opposition. Defensively, teams taught their offside middle-jamming defender (X3 in Diagram 5-4) that although their primary job was to stop the pass to the middle, they should be aware of this pass and to intercept it when possible.

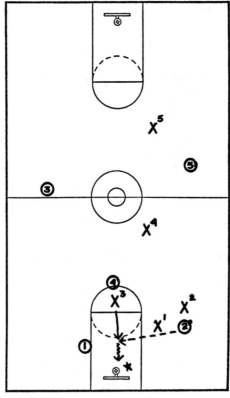

Diagram 5-4

Safe Reversal

The presence of a trailing big man ((3) in Diagram 5-5) allows for an easy safety-valve pass when the penetrating pass

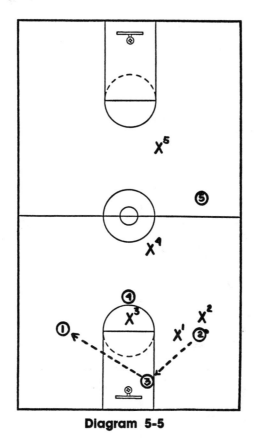

Diagram 5-5

from (2) to (4) cannot be made. The middle jammer X3 cannot cover this backwards pass and still protect his primary area (the middle).

As shown in Diagram 5-5 above, this pass to (3) leads to an easy, safe, reversal pass to (1).

Second Side

Getting the ball to the second side puts great pressure on the defense. A strong full-court zone press attempts to have all five defenders on the ball-side. This reversal forces all five defenders to make long slides and, at the same time, change assignments. Offensively, (4) then cuts to the ball-side, and (5) to the middle (Diagram 5-6). If player (1) can then get the ball to (5), player (2) will be open going up his sideline. See Diagram 5-7.

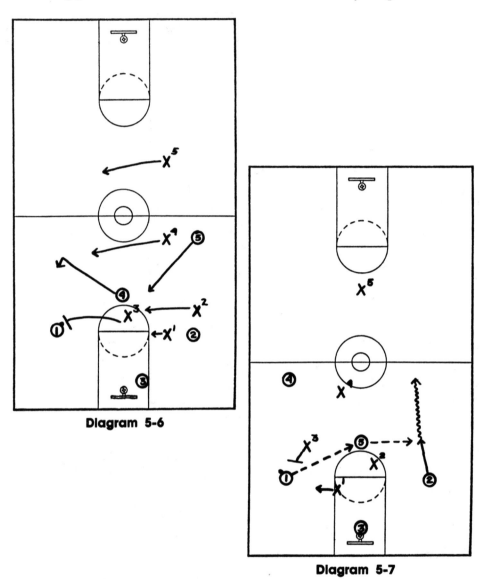

Diagram 5-6

Diagram 5-7

If (1) cannot get the ball to (5) (or to (4)), the possibility of another *quick* reversal by way of (3) to (2) still exists.

Anytime the ball is reversed by way of (3), he can further complicate the problems of the defense by faking to one side and throwing to the other. See Diagrams 5-8 and 5-9.

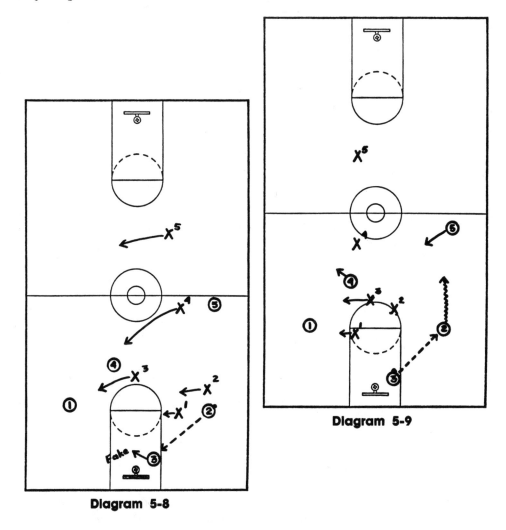

Diagram 5-9

Diagram 5-8

Proper Spacing

The coach must stress that this pattern requires proper spacing. Since no one goes downcourt to elongate the press, the defensive safety can play very high. To overcome this problem, the first pass (inbounds pass) must be made as high as the free throw line extended. This provides plenty of room for the backwards pass to (3). Players (4) and (5) should play as close to the midcourt line as possible. It might be wise for them to go all

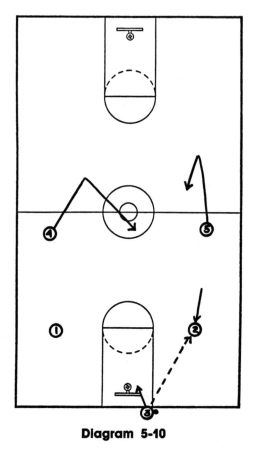

Diagram 5-10

the way to the frontcourt as the ball is inbounded and then come back to the ball. See Diagram 5-10.

The presence of the trailing big man forces the zone press to make adjustments which might open up the middle and result in easy baskets.

MOVING PATTERN ZONE PRESS—OFFENSE 1

Inbounding the Ball

The moving pattern also starts with (3), the agile big man, making the inbounds pass. Guards (1) and (2) attempt to get open as midcourt men (4) and (5) move to the frontcourt and then "V cut" back to the ball. In Diagram 5-11, (3) chooses to

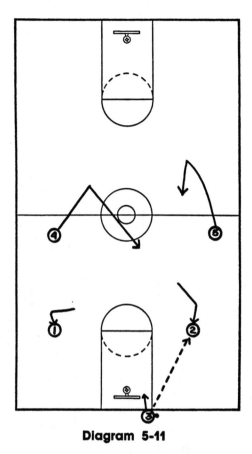

Diagram 5-11

pass to guard (2). Player (3) then steps inbounds and the offside midcourt man (4) cuts to the middle.

Pass to the Middle or Lob

On (4)'s cut to the middle, player (1) starts down the offside and may receive a lob pass from (2) (Diagram 5-12) or a reverse pass by way of (2) and (4) (Diagram 5-13). If (2) can pass to neither (4) nor (1), he looks for (3) or (5).

Pass to (5)

If the pass is made to (5), player (4) clears the middle and the offside midcourt man (now (1)) cuts to the middle, receives a pass, and looks for (3) on the weak side. See Diagrams 5-14 and 5-15.

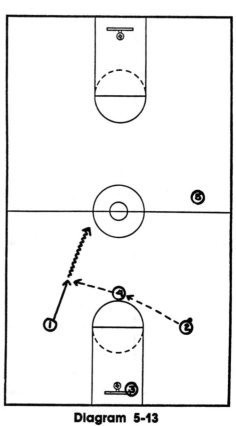

Diagram 5-13

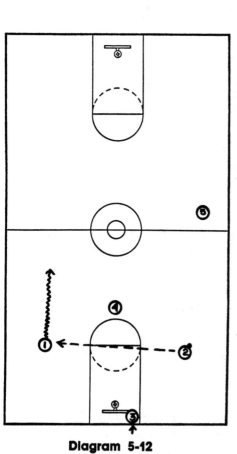

Diagram 5-12

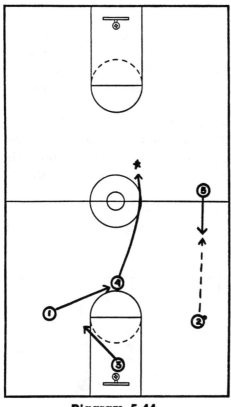

Diagram 5-14

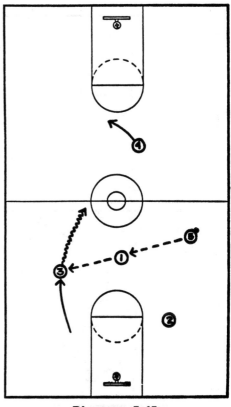

Diagram 5-15

Pass to (3)

If (2) would have chosen to pass to player (3), (4) would still have cleared the middle and the offside midcourt man (5) would have filled it (Diagram 5-16). Then if (3) passes to the middle, player (2) cuts down the weak side for a pass from (3). See Diagram 5-17.

This moving pattern makes denying the pass to the middle virtually impossible. The middle is constantly being cleared and new cutters move in. Once the ball is passed to the middle, the ball is reversed to the weak side and brought up-court with little opposition.

It should be noted that in the previous pattern, the middle man always cleared downcourt. In moving pattern 2, the middle man clears up-court.

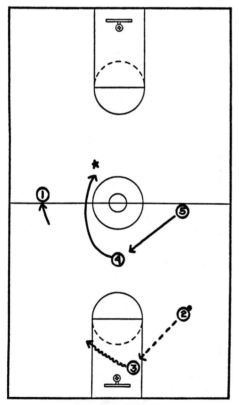

Diagram 5-16

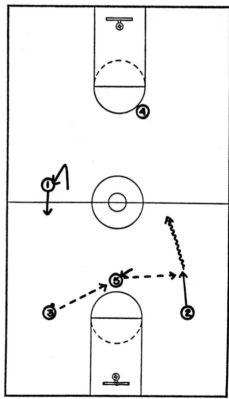

Diagram 5-17

MOVING PATTERN ZONE PRESS—OFFENSE 2

Inbounding the Ball

The ball is inbounded in the same manner as the previous patterns. The man receiving the inbounds pass ((2) in Diagram 5-18) has the options of lobbing crosscourt to (1) or reversing it to (1) by way of a pass to player (4).

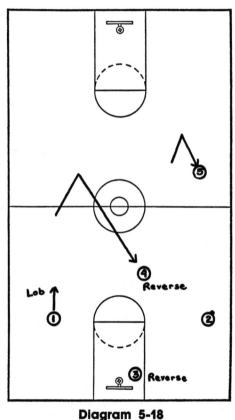

Diagram 5-18

Reversal

Since neither (1) nor (4) is open, (2) passes back to (3) who takes the ball to the weak side by way of the dribble (Diagram 5-19). This pass tells (5) to cut to the middle and (4) to clear. This time, however, player (4) clears to a position between and

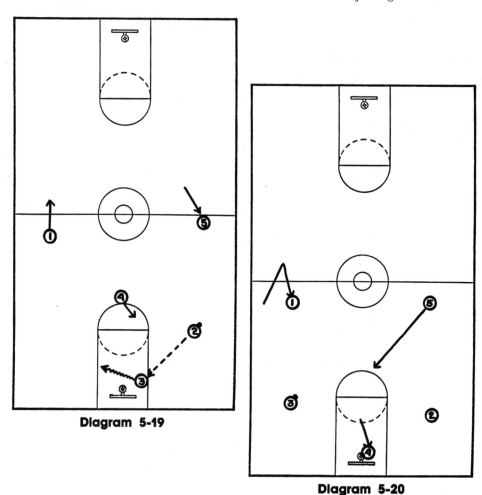

Diagram 5-19

Diagram 5-20

behind players (3) and (2) (Diagram 5-20). Player (3) may then lob to (2), reverse it to him by way of (5), or pass to (1) at midcourt (Diagram 5-21). If none of these options is available, (3) passes to (4), who takes the ball to the weak side to key player (5) to clear and (1) to take the middle. See Diagram 5-22.

These two moving patterns are attempts to overcome the zone press's ability to cover the middle. Having a trailing big man allows for a method of reversing the ball without forcing the dangerous pass to the middle. These patterns will force zone presses to make new adjustments.

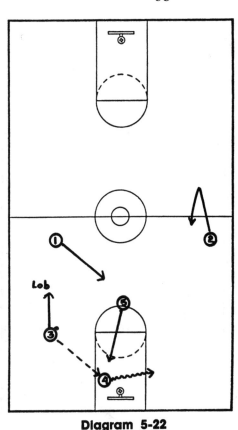

Diagram 5-22

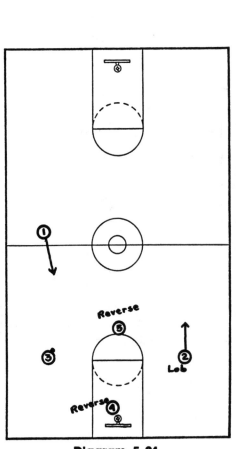

Diagram 5-21

Moving Pattern Zone Offenses Versus the 2-2-1 Press

A further advantage of these patterns can be found in their 1-2-2 shape. One of today's most popular zone presses is the 2-2-1 UCLA press. The defensive guards (X1 and X2) take your two guards head-on and attempt to force them into traps and turnovers. They are supported at mid-court by two trap-

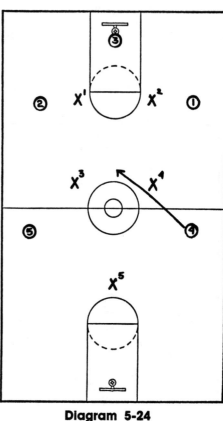

Diagram 5-24

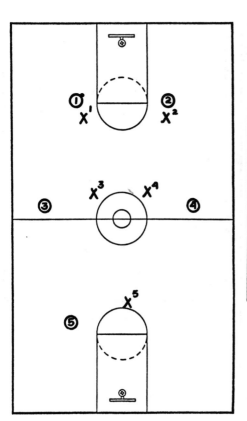

Diagram 5-23

pers (X3 and X4) and the fifth man (X5) acts as safety man. This defense is particularly effective against two-guard offenses. See Diagram 5-23.

The 1-2-2 shaped offense splits the 2-2-1, sends cutters into its middle, allows for easy reversal with the trailer, and destroys its basic function of harassing the two offensive guards by playing them in an almost man-to-man fashion. See Diagram 5-24.

A ZONE OR MAN-TO-MAN FULL-COURT-PRESS PATTERN

This full-court-press pattern is motion-oriented and may be used versus zone or man-to-man-pressure defenses.

Personnel Alignment

Agile forward (3) takes the ball out at the baseline and midway between the basket and sideline. Guards (1) and (2) stack and then each cuts to a side. Big men (4) and (5) race to mid-court and come back toward the ball. See Diagram 5-25.

Player (3) may pass to either guard ((1) or (2)) and then cut off the other and downcourt ((3)passes to (1) in Diagram 5-26). Guard (2) attempts to force a switch and end up with (3)'s

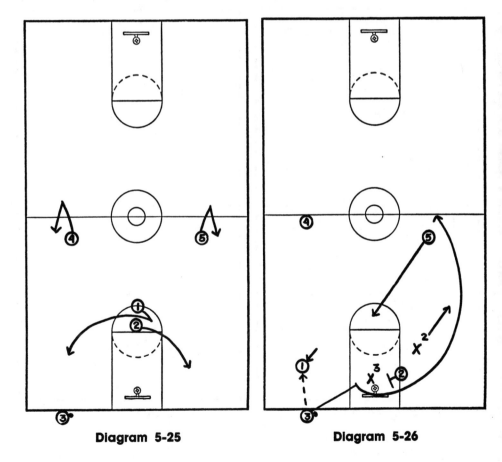

Diagram 5-25   Diagram 5-26

defender X3, who is taller and less agile than X2. Offside big man (5) cuts to the middle.

Three Basic Options

Player (1) has three choices. He may:

A. Try to get the ball to (5) in the middle and cut off a screen by (4). If this pass is made, it serves (on the weak side) as a backdoor play key versus man-to-man defenses, and a weak side reversal versus zone presses. See Diagram 5-27.

B. Upon receiving the inbounds pass, throw the ball to (4) on his side. When he does this, (5) cuts to the middle

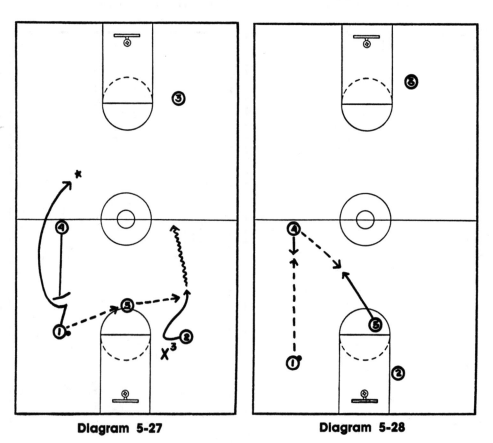

Diagram 5-27   **Diagram 5-28**

and (4) passes to him (Diagram 5-28). Player (1) waits for (4)'s pass to (5) and cuts off of the subsequent screen (by (4)), and (2) takes the reversal (or backdoor) pass and brings the ball up-court. See Diagram 5-29.

C. If, after the inbounds pass, player (1) cannot get the ball to (5) in the middle or (4) on the sideline, he passes to player (2). This pass tells (5) to cut to his side and (4) to take the middle. Players (1) and (2) must be aware that this pass is a dangerous one; (1) must pass it briskly and (2) must come to meet the ball (Diagram 5-30). Player (2) then passes to (4) in the middle and cuts off (5) and up-court. Player (4) then passes to (1) and this amounts

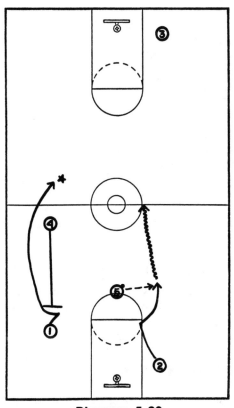

Diagram 5-29

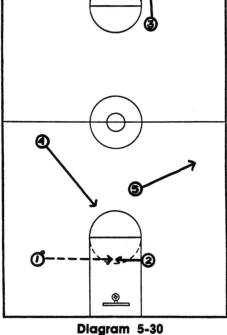

Diagram 5-30

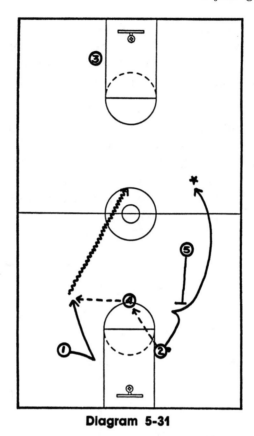

Diagram 5-31

to a backdoor versus man-to-man and a weak side reverse against zone-pressure defenses. See Diagram
5-31.

The fact that a weak side-reversal play (versus zones) and a
backdoor play (versus man-to-man) involve the same player
passes and cuts makes this pattern functional against either
type pressure defense.

THE MULTIPURPOSE PATTERN

I first learned how to beat the zone press by reading Ed
Jucker's great book *Power Basketball*. In it, he details a full-court
pattern and also a separate pattern to defeat half-court zone
presses.

Basic Rules

After using both patterns, we finally decided to use his half-court pattern against both full- and half-court presses. It was a 2-1-2 pattern with the following rules:

1. The onside forward plays up and the offside forward down.
2. When the ball goes in the middle, both forwards run for the basket and the offside guard goes down the weak side looking for a pass from the middle man.
3. Get the ball into the middle whenever possible.

Rules in Action

Following are the rules in action versus a full-court press:

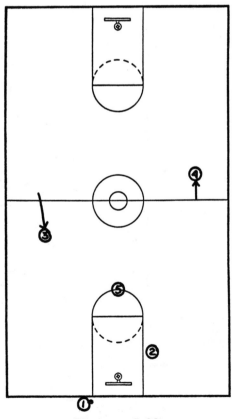

Diagram 5-32

Player (3) is the onside (ball side) forward and he plays up; (4) is the offside forward and he is downcourt. See Diagram 5-32.

(1)'s pass to (2) reverses (3) and (4)'s assignments. See Diagram 5-33.

When (2) makes a pass to the middle, both forwards go downcourt and the offside guard goes down the weak side; (2) is the safety man. See Diagram 5-34.

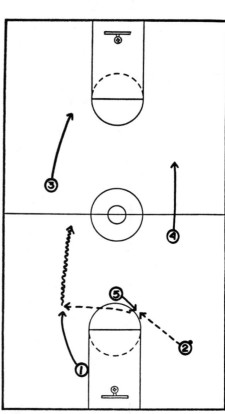

Diagram 5-34

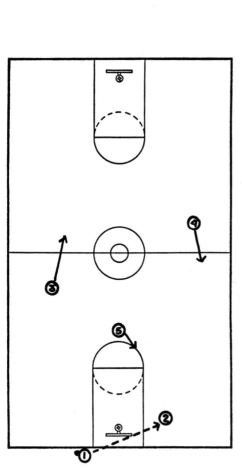

Diagram 5-33

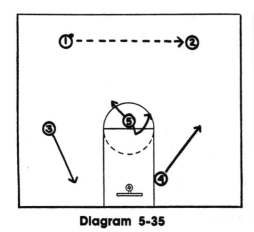
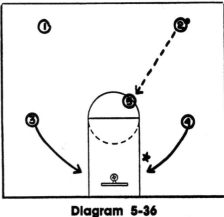

Diagram 5-35   **Diagram 5-36**

Following are the same rules versus half-court press:

Player (1) passes to (2); (3) and (4) change assignments (Diagram 5-35). The ball goes into the middle. Forwards (3) and (4) run for the basket and the offside guard (1) goes down the weak side. See Diagram 5-36.

Note: When the ball is passed guard to forward, the forward attempts to get it in the middle and the same rules prevail.

Pulling Out Zones

We used the same pattern to pull zones out and then attempt to penetrate them. These are the rules in action versus a 2-3 zone.

The onside forward (3) is up and the offside forward (4) is down. See Diagram 5-37.

A guard-to-guard pass changes (3) and (4)'s assignments. See Diagram 5-38.

When the ball goes into the middle, both forwards (3) and (4) run to the basket. The offside guard (1) moves down the weak side and is usually open. See Diagram 5-39.

When using this pattern against zones, stay wide, move the ball, and make them come out to cover you.

Using this pattern in three situations makes the game less complicated for the players, makes the coach's teaching assignment easier, and conserves valuable practice time.

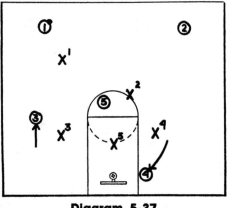

Diagram 5-37

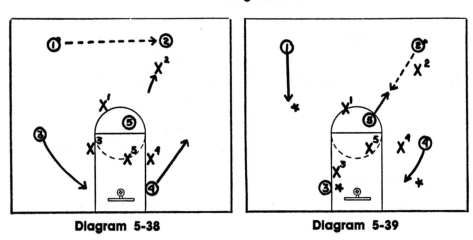

Diagram 5-38   **Diagram 5-39**

These four patterns offer enough variety that most coaches can find one that fits their personnel; they also have new concepts that will force the zone pressure team to amend their full-court plan and make new adjustments.

Ball-Control Techniques

six

For a long time basketball was a fast-breaking, free-flowing, high-scoring game. However, coaches have discovered that a team that practices ball control and fastidious shot selection may have an advantage over the running team. Ray Mears, the former great Tennessee coach and a practitioner of disciplined control basketball, once pointed out to me that it is very advantageous to force your opponents to spend a lot of time on defense because:

1. Players commit most of their fouls on defense.
2. Defense is more tiring than offense.
3. At the conclusion of any close game, both teams attempt to "set it up" and work for good shots.

In the past, delays and stalls were used primarily to kill the clock and protect the lead at the end of close games. Now, they may be interjected at any point in the game. The technique has been very successful and this success may be due to the simple fact that although being tall is an attribute in many facets of the game, it is a handicap when the opposition chooses to play "keep away." This tight-fisted era of basketball will probably end with the installation of the shot clock, but as of now, a team must possess ball-control techniques and be able to execute them in a disciplined manner.

The following four offenses may be used to make the opposition play defense or simply take time off the clock.

THE FLEX SEMISTALL

The flex continuity may be used as a semistall or delay game by adding two options.

Personnel Alignment

This offense starts with a high-post man (5) and four interchangeable perimeter men. Players (1) and (2) start in the guard positions and (3) and (4) start in the forward area. See Diagram 6-1.

The basic plan has two delay options keyed by a guard-to-guard pass or a guard-to-forward pass. The scoring or flex option is keyed by a guard-to-high-post pass.

The Guard-to-Guard Pass

In Diagram 6-2, guard (1) passes to guard (2) and exchanges with the forward on his side, (3).

The Guard-to-Forward Pass

When a guard passes to the forward on his side (as (1) passed to (3) in Diagram 6-3), he then cuts over high-post man (5) for a possible lob pass. To clear that area, players (2) and (4) rotate toward the ball side.

If (3) cannot lob pass to (1), he passes out front to (2). See Diagram 6-4.

Dribble Chase

During these two delay options, the defense will often attempt to deny passes. When this occurs, a dribble chase may be used. Diagram 6-5 shows a guard-to-guard dribble chase and Diagram 6-6 shows a forward-to-guard dribble chase.

The rule to follow when someone dribbles at you is to cut to the basket and fill on the side of the floor from which the

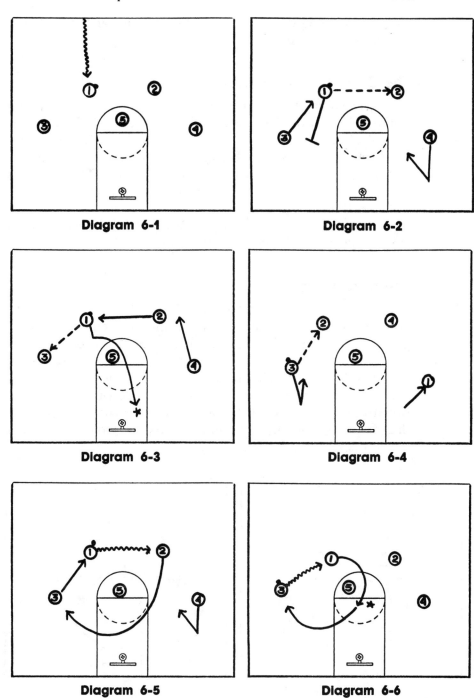

Diagram 6-1

Diagram 6-2

Diagram 6-3

Diagram 6-4

Diagram 6-5

Diagram 6-6

dribbler came. Other players should rotate toward the ball and fill one of the four offensive-perimeter spots.

The Guard-to-Post Pass

The Guard-to-Post pass keys the offense's basic scoring option which is the flex continuity. In Diagram 6-7, guard (1) passes to post man (5); guards (1) and (2) then exchange with their respective forwards. Player (5) may then pass to either (4) or (3). In Diagram 6-8, he chooses to pass to (3). This pass tells guard (2) to step up and blindscreen for (4) who cuts to the basket. See Diagram 6-8.

Player (5) then screens down for (2) and the flex continuity is in process. See Diagrams 6-9 through 6-11.

The Stall Phase

To convert this semistall into a full-scale stall, only one option is changed. The guard-to-guard option is retained as is the guard-to-forward option. But when a guard-to-post pass is made (as when (1) passed to (5) in Diagram 6-12), the result is a guard and forward exchange on each side of the court. To provide a possible scoring option and take some of the defensive pressure off the forwards ((3) and (4)), the forwards may backdoor before exchanging. Player (5) then passes to the open man and the stall goes on. See Diagram 6–13.

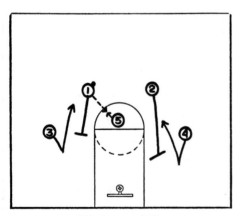

Diagram 6-7

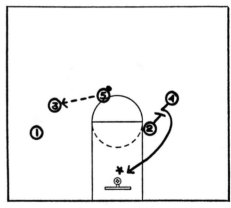

Diagram 6-8

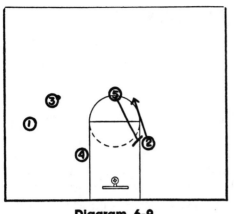

Diagram 6-9

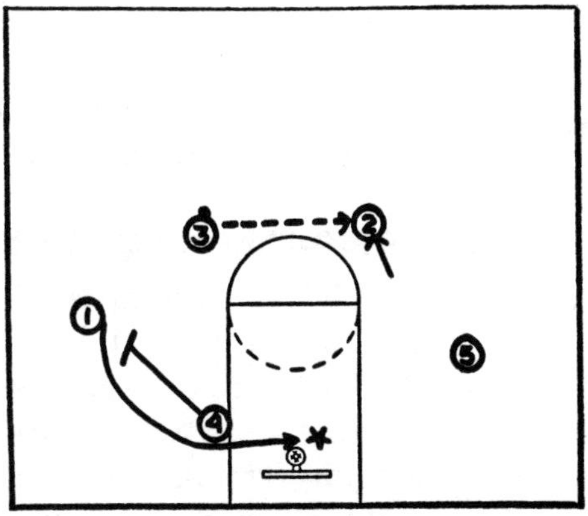

Diagram 6-10

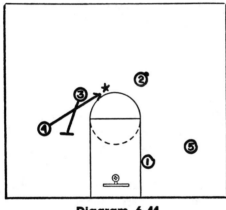

Diagram 6-11

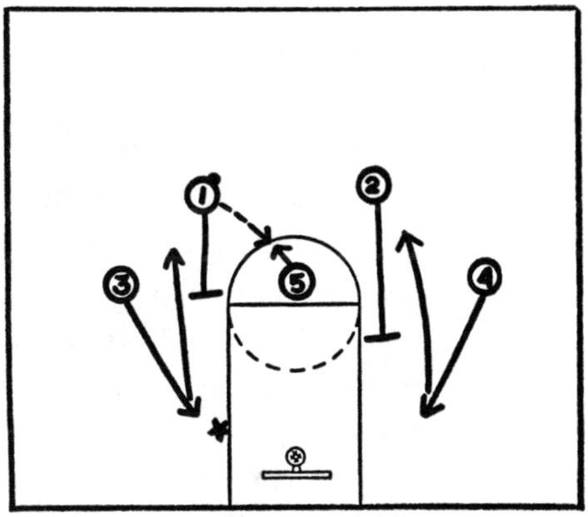

Diagram 6-12

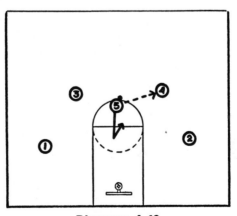

Diagram 6-13

THE UCLA SEMISTALL

The UCLA Semistall derives its name from the fact that its key scoring cut is the UCLA high-post slash maneuver.

Personnel Alignment

The two guards ((1) and (2)) play at least as wide as the free throw lane, and a step or two above the free throw circle. The forwards ((3) and (4)) also play wide and as high as the free throw line extended. In some cases, the guards and forwards are interchangeable so it helps if they have strong all-around skills. High-post man (5) is primarily a screener and rebounder, and seldom handles the ball. See Diagram 6-14.

This semistall offense also has two defense moving, clock killing plays and a basic scoring option.

The Two Clock Killers

Pass to the Post

When guard (1) passes to (5) (Diagram 6-15), both guards are keyed to cross, forward (3) goes backdoor, and forward (4) moves into the lane. Post man (5) looks first for forward (3) and then for guard (1), who has cut over forward (4) for a possible lay-up.

If neither (3) or (1) are open, forward (3) stops and then uses a screen by (2) to move out front. Player (4), after screening, rolls out front. The net result has been a guard and forward exchange. See Diagrams 6-16 and 6-17.

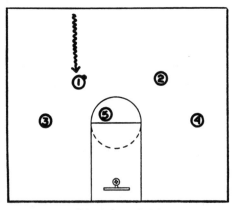

Diagram 6-14

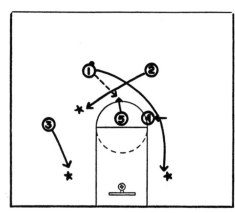

Diagram 6-15

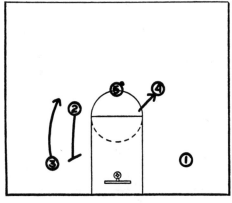

Diagram 6-16

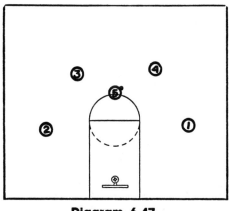

Diagram 6-17

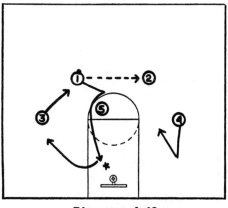

Diagram 6-18

The Guard-to-Guard Pass

In Diagram 6-18, guard (1) passes to (2), steps toward him, and then cuts off (5) for a possible lob pass. Forward (3) moves out front and the result is a guard-forward exchange away from the ball.

The Basic Scoring Option (Guard-to-Forward Pass)

When (1) passes to (3), he makes his UCLA slash cut off (5) to the ball-side low-post area. On the offside, guard (2) and forward (4) exchange; (4) then continues to the point. See Diagram 6-19.

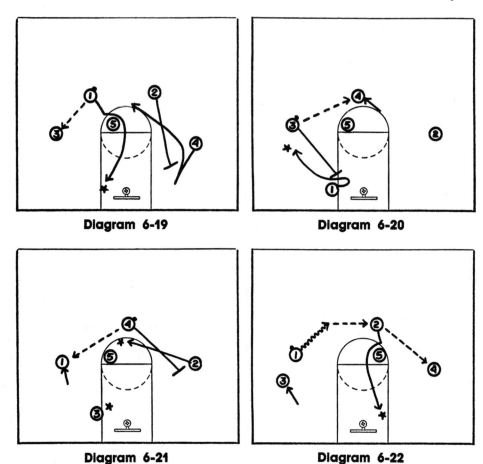

Diagram 6-19

Diagram 6-20

Diagram 6-21

Diagram 6-22

If (1) is not open on his slash cut, player (3) passes to (4) and downscreens for (1), who pops to the ball-side wing area (Diagram 6-20). Forward (4) may then do one of two things: He may, if (1) is open off (3)'s downscreen, pass to him and screen away for (2) (Diagram 6-21). Player (1) may shoot, pass to (3) inside, or take the ball back out front by passing to (2). Player (2) would then shoot or initiate a new series (Diagram 6-22); or he ((4)) may dribble toward and then pass to (2) as (1) comes out front, and then slash cut off (5) to initiate a new series. See Diagram 6-23.

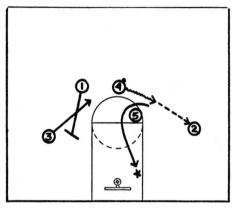

Diagram 6-23

The Stall Phase

To convert this semistall to a full-scale stall, only one option is changed. The guard-to-guard option is retained as is the guard-to-post option. But when a guard-to-forward option is keyed as the pass from (1) to (3) in Diagram 6-24, guard (1) makes his slash cut off (5); if he is open, (3) will pass to him.

If player (1) is not open, forward (3) dribbles out front, (1) replaces him at the wing, and a new option is keyed. See Diagram 6-25.

Whether using the semistall or complete-stall phase, the following play may be used to provide a high-percentage last-second shot. With 10 seconds remaining, your best shooter ((1) in Diagrams 6-24 and 6-25) passes to (3) and slash cuts off (5) and to the ball-side low-post area (Diagram 6-26). Player (3) then passes to (4), who has exchanged with (2) and moved to the point. See Diagram 6-27.

After passing to (4), player (3) joins (5) to form a double screen for (1). At the same time, (2) screens down for (1) on the other side. Guard (1) may then cut to either side for a jump shot. Diagram 6-28 shows (1) using (3) and (5)'s double screen. Diagram 6-29 shows (1) faking a cut around the double screen and using (2) to get open.

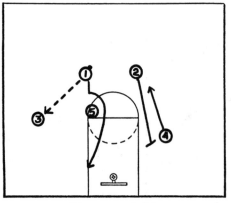

Diagram 6-24

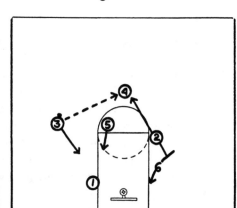

Diagram 6-25

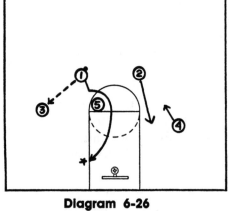

Diagram 6-26

Diagram 6-27

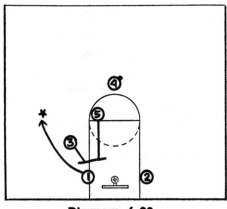

Diagram 6-28

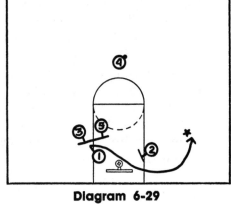

Diagram 6-29

A 1-3-1 ALL-PURPOSE OFFENSE

This offense may be used as a semistall disciplined control game, as a complete stall, or as a zone offense.

Personnel Alignment

Point man (1) is the primary ball handler who must bring the ball up-court and initiate the motion. Once the play has started, (1)'s job is interchangeable with players (2), (3), and (4); (5)'s job consists mostly of screening and being the primary rebounder. See Diagram 6-30.

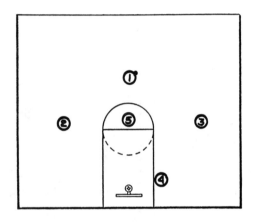

Diagram 6-30

The Basic Motion
of the Disciplined Control Offense

Point man (1) may pass to either wing (as to (2) in Diagram 6-31) and then cut off (5) to the ball-side low-post area; (4) will fill the offside corner. Player (3) then cuts to the point, (4) re-places him, and (1) clears to the ball-side corner. See Diagram 6-32.

The ball is then reversed to (4) by way of (3). Player (3) then cuts off high-post man (5) and the offside players ((1) and (2)) fill the open spots. See Diagrams 6-33 and 6-34.

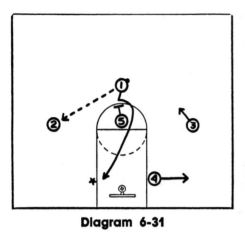

Diagram 6-31

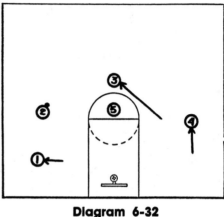

Diagram 6-32

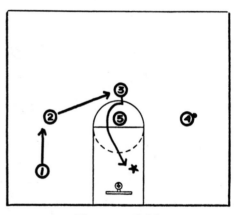

Diagram 6-33

Diagram 6-34

Pressure Relievers

When defensive pressure is being exerted on the perimeter passes, these pressure-relieving options may be run.

Pressure on the Wing-to-Point Pass

In Diagram 6-35, wing man (2) cannot get the ball to (3) at the point because X2 is denying the pass. This inability to pass tells (5) to break to the ball and receive a pass from (2); (2) may then: screen for (1); this screen will tell (3) to backdoor his de-

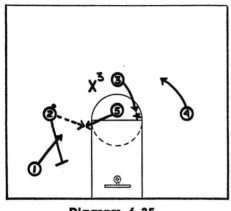

Diagram 6-35

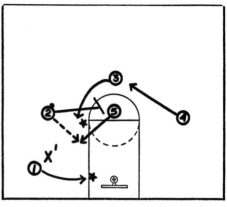

Diagram 6-36

fender; or screen for (3), and (1) will backdoor. See Diagram 6-36.

This play also works very well to obtain a last-second shot.

Pressure on the Point-to-Wing Pass

In Diagram 6-37, point man (3) cannot pass to (4) because X4 is denying the pass.

When (4) is covered, (2) will screen down for (1) who will move to the wing. Player (2) will then clear to the far corner and the continuity will go on. See Diagrams 6-38 and 6-39.

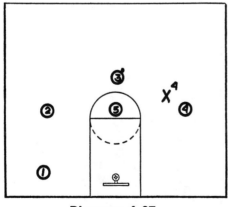

Diagram 6-37

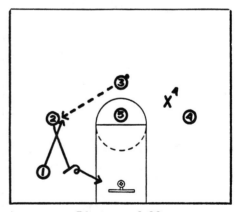

Diagram 6-38

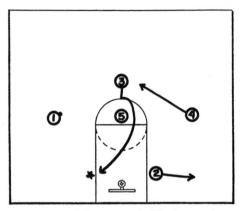

Diagram 6-39

Using the 1-3-1 All-Purpose Offense as a Stall

When using this offense as a complete stall, the same basic motion is used, but to relieve pass-denying pressure, dribble chases, followed by perimeter rotations, are used. Diagrams 6-40 and 6-41 show a dribble chase and perimeter rotation when the wing-to-point ((3) to (1)) pass is denied.

Diagrams 6-42 and 6-43 show a dribble chase and perimeter rotation when the point (1) to wing (3) pass is denied.

If a pass to the post man ((5)) becomes necessary during the stall phase, it would key a double exchange. Diagram 6-44 shows point man (1) passing to post man (5) and exchanging

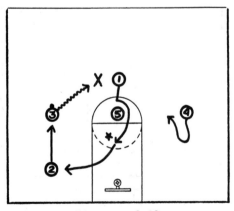

Diagram 6-40

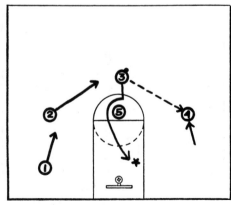

Diagram 6-41

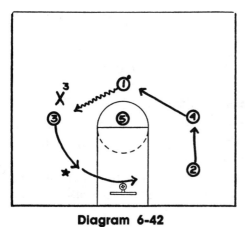

Diagram 6-42

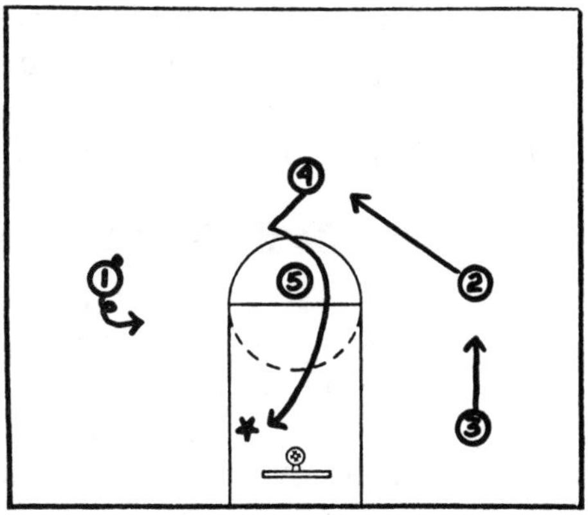

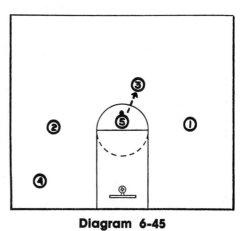

Diagram 6-43

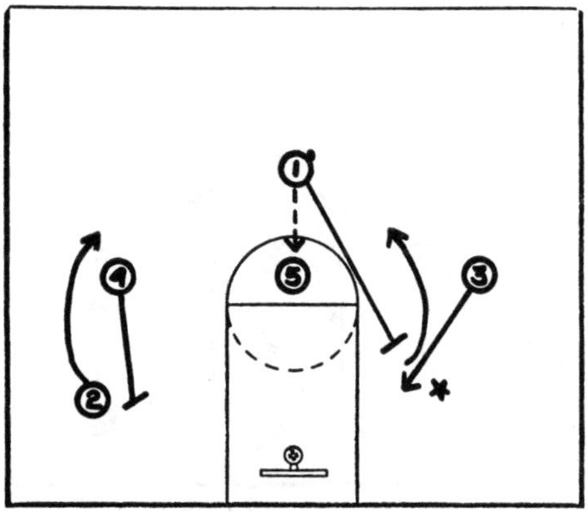

Diagram 6-44

Diagram 6-45

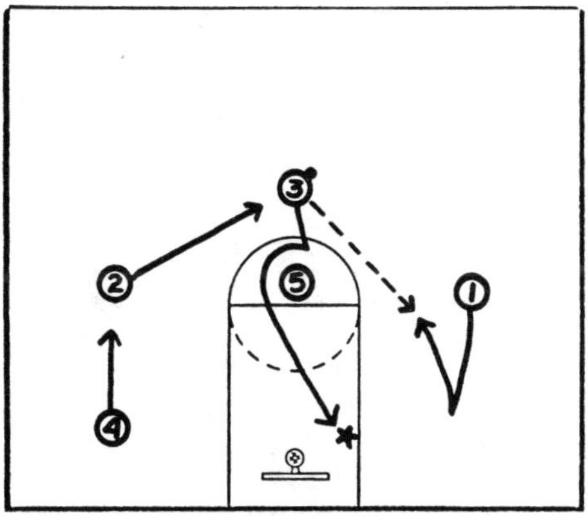

Diagram 6-46

with wing man (3). At the same time, wing man (4) would exchange with corner man (2).

Player (5) then returns the ball to the perimeter and the basic continuity is run. See Diagrams 6-45 and 6-46.

The Basic Motion Versus Zones

When this motion is run versus zones, it consists of overloading one side, and moving the ball to utilize the overload passing triangles. See Diagram 6-47.

The point man is the only player who can switch the side of the overload. He does this by passing to the weak side and

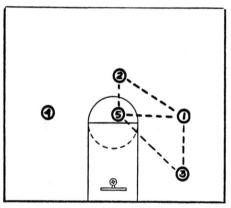

Diagram 6-47

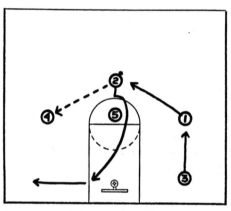

Diagram 6-48

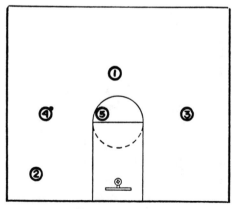

Diagram 6-49

cutting through to the ball-side corner. See this overload switch keyed by (2) in Diagrams 6-48 and 6-49.

The overload-passing triangles would then be utilized until new point man (1) decides to switch the overload.

A THREE-PHASE GUARD-OPTION CONTROL GAME

This disciplined control game is a combination of two well-established offenses. It may be used as a quick-hitting, catch-up offense, as a complete stall, or as a disciplined control game. Each play is keyed by the front man with the ball. This offense is very difficult to defense because the guard options provide a great deal of spontaneity.

Personnel Alignment

The four perimeter players are interchangeable and the high-post man (5) must be a strong ball handler, but doesn't need to be very tall. The offense starts from a two-guard, two-forward, high-post alignment. See Diagram 6-50.

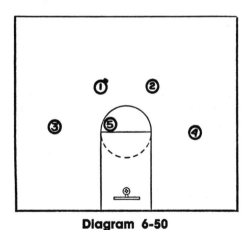

Diagram 6-50

The Quick-Hitting Catch-Up Offense

This phase of the offensive plan is used when you are behind and need quick shots to catch up. The three options of the offense are: the guard-to-guard pass, the guard-to-forward pass, and the guard-to-post pass.

Guard-to-Guard Pass

In Diagram 6-51, guard (1) passes to guard (2), then cuts over post man (5) to the ball-side low-post area. Player (5) then pops out and receives a pass from (2), who cuts down the lane. Forward (3) screens down for (1), who has cut across the lane, and forward (4) screens down for (2). See Diagram 6-52.

Forwards (3) and (4) then post up and (5) passes to the open man. See Diagram 6-53.

If no one has a shot, player (5) passes to (1) or (2) and they bring the ball out front as (5) returns to his original position. See Diagram 6-54.

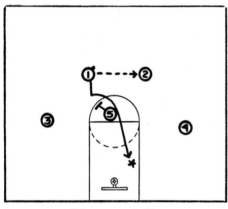

Diagram 6-51

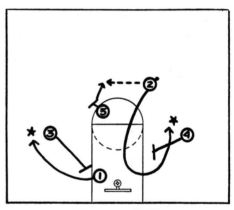

Diagram 6-52

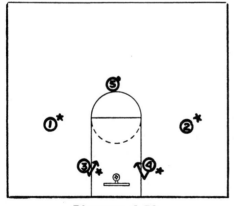

Diagram 6-53

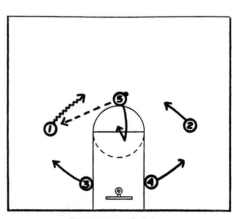

Diagram 6-54

Guard-to-Forward Pass

This time, (1) passes to (3), the forward on his side. Players (1) and (2) then cut down and across the lane to receive downscreens from the forward on that side. Forward (3) passes to (5) popping out before screening down for (2) (Diagrams 6-55 and 6-56). Players (3) and (4) again post up, and (5) passes to the open man.

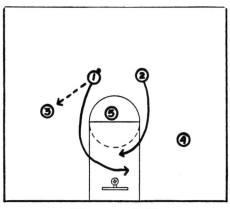

Diagram 6-55

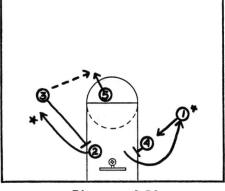

Diagram 6-56

Guard-to-Post Pass

This time (1) passes to (5). He and (2) cut down and cross, while (3) and (4) again screen down. Players (1) and (2) then pop out, and (3) and (4) post up; (5) passes to the open man. See Diagram 6-57.

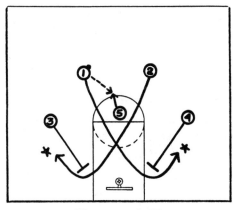

Diagram 6-57

Remember that this is the quick-hitting, catch-up phase of the offense.

The Stalling Phase

This time, (1) again may key the offense by a guard-to-guard pass, a guard-to-forward pass, or a guard-to-post pass. The idea in this phase is to hold the ball. This is done by way of numerous guard and forward exchanges.

Guard-to-Guard Pass

Guard (1) passes to (2) and screens down for his forward (3), who moves out front. See Diagram 6-58.

Guard-to-Forward Pass

Guard (1) passes to (3) and cuts to the ball-side corner; (3) then dribbles out front. See Diagrams 6-59 and 6-60.

Note that (2) and (4) exchanged on the offside.

Guard-to-Post Pass

Guard (1) passes to post man (5), and the guards ((1) and (2)) and the forwards ((3) and (4)) exchange positions. See Diagram 6-61.

These exchanges and pass options permit the team to stall the ball. Any scoring is done because of defensive mistakes and/or by way of individual player initiative.

The Basic Disciplined Control Offense Phase

The basic offense is used the vast majority of the time and is a combination of the stall and quick-hitting phases. The ball-side front man (1) again keys the play and, in this case, the other players must be very alert to read them correctly.

The Guard-to-Guard Pass

In Diagram 6-62, guard (1) passes to guard (2) and may cut over (5) to key a scoring option, or go directly to screen (3) and key a delay option (Diagram 6-63).

The other four players must watch (1)'s cut and then react to it.

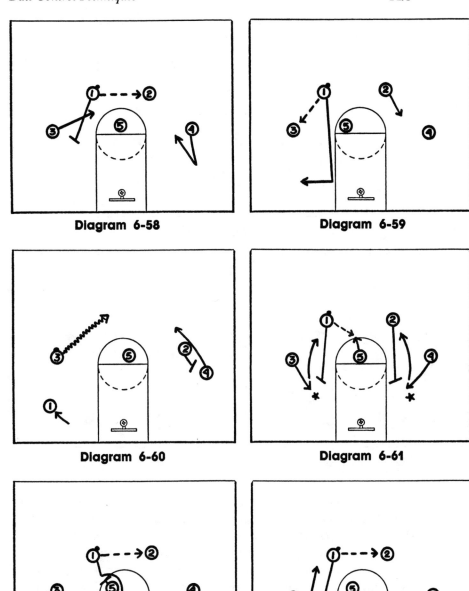

Diagram 6-58

Diagram 6-59

Diagram 6-60

Diagram 6-61

Diagram 6-62

Diagram 6-63

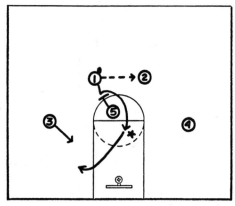

Diagram 6-64

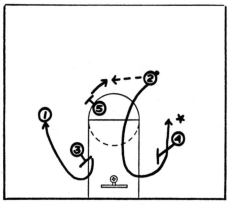

Diagram 6-65

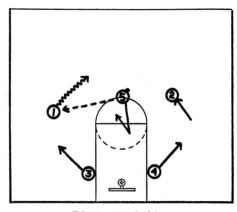

Diagram 6-66

Obviously (as shown in Diagram 6-63), after the delay option, the team is in position to run another option. However, the same holds true after the scoring option. Diagrams 6-64 and 6-65 show the guard-to-guard scoring option.

If this option did not provide a shot, (5) passes to one of the guards ((1) in Diagram 6-66) and returns to his original position. Guard (1) brings the ball out front and any of the options may be run.

The Guard-to-Forward Pass

This time guard (1) passes to (3) (the forward on his side) and may: Cut down and across the lane to key a scoring option

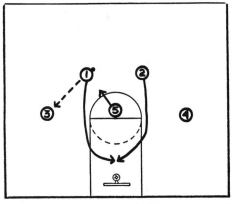

Diagram 6-67

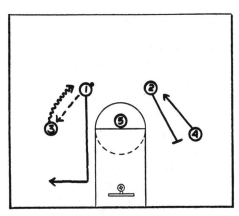

Diagram 6-68

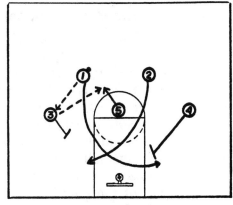

Diagram 6-69

(see Diagram 6-67), or cut to the ball-side corner and key a de-laying option (see Diagram 6-68).

The other players must observe (1)'s cut and make the proper response to it.

Again it is obvious that the delay option will conclude with the players in position to run any of the options. However, the same holds true after the scoring option of the guard-to-forward play. For example, in Diagrams 6-69 and 6-70, the scoring option is run.

If a shot was not forthcoming, (5) would pass to a guard ((2) in Diagram 6-71), who would bring the ball out front and key a new option.

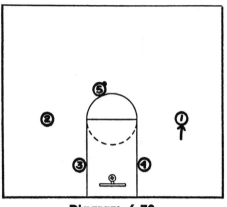

Diagram 6-70

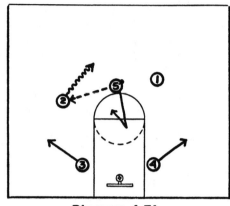

Diagram 6-71

The Guard-to-Post Play

This time guard (1) passes to post man (5) and may key a stall or scoring option. In Diagram 6-72, (1) passes to (5) and keys a scoring option by cutting across the lane.

Player (1) could have passed to (5) and keyed a stall option, setting a definite screen for (3). See Diagram 6-73.

Note that in either case, the other players must observe (1)'s cut and make the proper responses.

Again, it is apparent that after the stall option, the team is in position to run a new play. It is also apparent at the conclusion of the guard-to-post scoring option. Diagrams 6-74 and 6-75 show the scoring option being run.

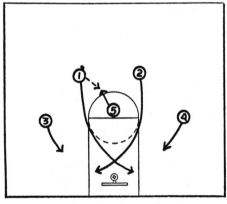

Diagram 6-72

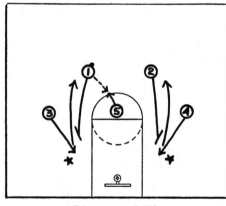

Diagram 6-73

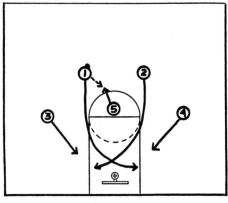

Diagram 6-74

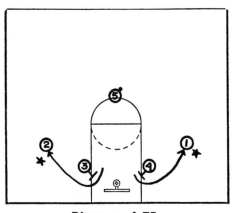

Diagram 6-75

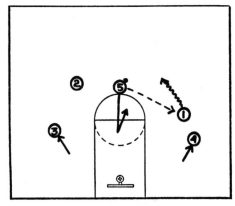

Diagram 6-76

If nothing develops, (5) would pass to a guard ((1) in Diagram 6-76), who would bring the ball out front and key the next option.

By interchanging the three scoring options and three stalling options, the offense can really probe the defense. The stalling options test the patience and discipline of the defenders. As soon as they relax, a scoring option may lead to an easy basket.

These four offenses are designed to force the opposition to spend a lot of time on defense. They are versatile in that they may be used in multiple situations.

Versatile Out-of-Bounds Plays

seven

Coaching strategy and rule changes have increased the importance of out-of-bounds plays. Coaches save their time-outs and use them to set up last-minute defensive plans that deny and/or trap the inbounds pass. At various levels of competition, out-of-bounds situations have replaced free throws and jump ball plays due to rule changes. The end result is more out-of-bounds plays against tougher defenses. These tougher defenses make an extensive repertoire of out-of-bounds plays a necessity. Following are out-of-bounds plays to be used at the frontcourt baseline, frontcourt sideline, backcourt baseline, and backcourt sideline.

The out-of-bounds plays that follow should be examined in terms of their mechanical efficiency, how they fit your team's personnel, and how out-of-bounds plays are defensed in your league.

OUT-OF-BOUNDS PLAYS UNDER THE BASKET

The Vertical Lineup Series

This series is a three-play plan keyed by (2), the player across the lane from the vertical lineup. It may be used versus man-to-man or zone defenses. The three plays are: the Shoot the Gap, the Screen and Roll, and the Back Out.

129

Shoot the Gap

Player (2) cuts across the lane and through the gap between (3) and (4) at the bottom of the vertical stack. Player (3) may be able to force a switch by screening (2)'s man on this cut and then roving inside the defense. Player (5) reads (2)'s cut and then fakes outside and comes down the lane. See Diagram 7-1.

If a shot is not forthcoming, player (1) passes to (2), then loops around (4) and (3) to the point. Player (2) passes to (1) after looking inside to (3). Player (4) moves down to screen for (1) and then rolls across the lane and around (5). See Diagram 7-2.

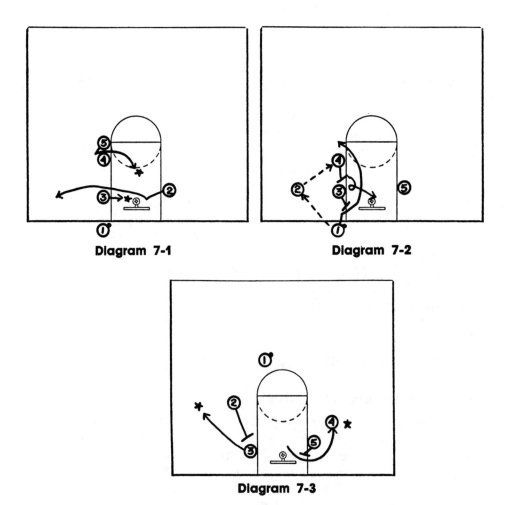

Diagram 7-1   Diagram 7-2

Diagram 7-3

Player (1) can then pass to (4) moving around (5)'s downscreen. If (4) is not open, player (2) screens down for (3) who pops out for a possible jump shot. See Diagram 7-3.

The Screen and Roll

Player (2) moves across the lane and sets a definite screen for (3) who goes the opposite way across the lane. Player (2) rolls inside and (1) may pass to either the screener (2) or cutter (3). Player (5) reads this key and cuts to the ball-side corner. See Diagram 7-4.

If the screen and roll does not provide a shot, player (1) passes to (5) and loops out to the point (Diagram 7-5). Player (4) again loops around the offside man and (5) screens down for (2). See Diagram 7-6.

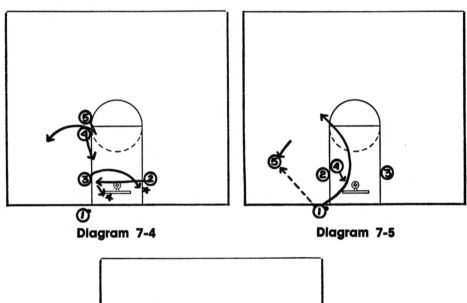

Diagram 7-4   Diagram 7-5

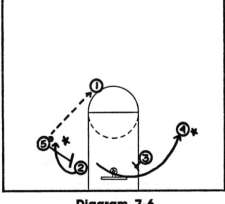

Diagram 7-6

The Backout Play

Player (2) backs out to the far corner, which keys (4) and (3) to move up and screen (5)'s defender X5. Player (5) cuts to the basket and may receive a lob pass on the way, or move all the way to the basket for a power lay-up. See Diagram 7-7. If (5) is not open, (4) cuts back to the ballside corner and (3) rolls down the lane (Diagram 7-8). Player (1) takes a quick look at (3), and if he is not open, (1) passes to (4), and then loops to the point. See Diagram 7-9.

Player (4) then passes to (1) after looking inside for (5). Player (3) loops around (2), who downscreens, and (4) also screens down for (5), who pops to the wing. See Diagram 7-10.

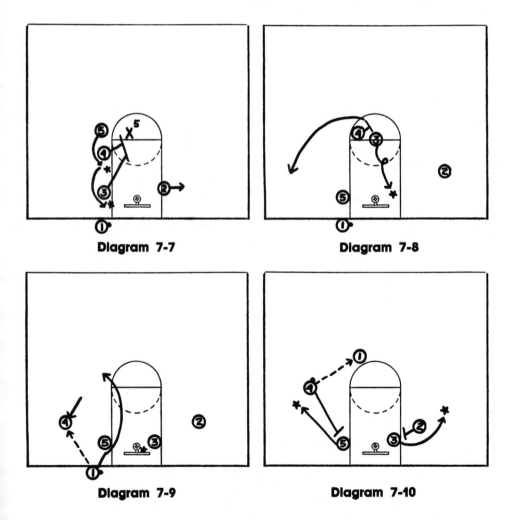

Diagram 7-7   Diagram 7-8

Diagram 7-9   Diagram 7-10

In general, the screen and roll options of these three plays are designed for man-to-man defense and the perimeter reversal phase is best against zones.

SIDE OUT-OF-BOUNDS PLAY (FRONTCOURT)

If the opposition chooses to play zone defense versus side out-of-bounds plays, it is best to pass the ball in and run your zone offense. However, if they decide to play a denying man-to-man, the following plays may be run.

The High Double Stack

The ball is taken out by forward (4) in Diagram 7-11. Player (2) initiates the movement by clearing his man to the backcourt. This motion tells guard (1) to step up and screen for (3), who cuts to the basket for a possible lob pass.

It is possible that (3) may be open for the lob. But the real reasons for this movement were to clear (2) and his defender, and allow (1) to get open by forcing a switch by X3 and X1; he ((1)) then pops toward the ball. Once the pass is made from (4) to (1), player (5) slides down and (4) uses him as a natural screen as he ((4)) cuts to the basket. See Diagram 7-12.

If (4) is not open, he loops around (3) (Diagram 7-13); then loops around post man (5), player (2) moves down, and the team is in their 2-3 set and is ready to run the offense. See Diagram 7-14.

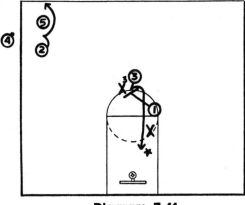

Diagram 7-11

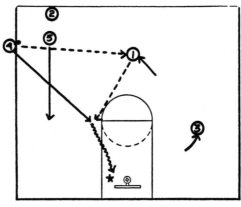

Diagram 7-12

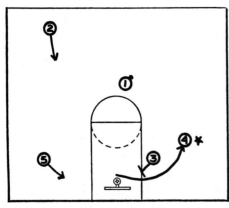

Diagram 7-13

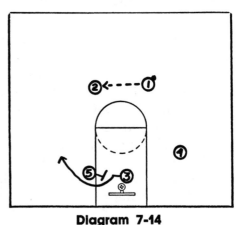

Diagram 7-14

The Low Double-Stack Sideline Out-of-Bound Play

This play begins with guard (1) taking the ball out on the sideline, and the other players forming a double stack on each side of the free throw lane. The offside stack should contain the team's best inside player (5), and the team's best all-around player (3). See Diagram 7-15.

The play begins as (2) pops out of his stack and to the ball-side point. Player (1) passes to him and moves toward the free throw lane. See Diagram 7-16.

From there, the option that occurs will depend on (3). The options are the Stack Option and the Portland Option.

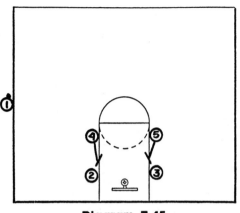

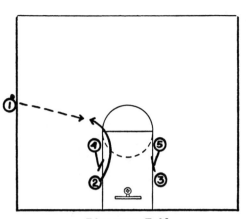

Diagram 7-15   **Diagram 7-16**

Stack Option

In Diagram 7-17, player (3) waits until (2) receives his pass from (1) and looks at him ((3)). Then he pops out of (5)'s downscreen. Player (2) passes to (3), who may shoot or pass to (5) inside.

In many cases, X5 will front (5). To take advantage of this fact, (1) breaks to the high-post area when he sees that (3) can't shoot or pass to (5). Player (1) may receive a pass from (3) and find (5) inside of X5 for a power lay-up shot. See Diagram 7-18.

This play works equally well against zone defenses.

If player (3) cannot pass to (5) or (1), player (4) moves up to blind-screen for (2); (2) then cuts to the basket looking for a lob pass from (3). See Diagram 7-19.

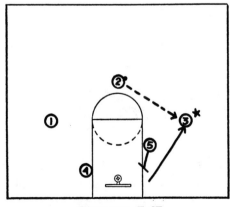

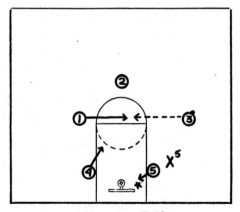

Diagram 7-17   **Diagram 7-18**

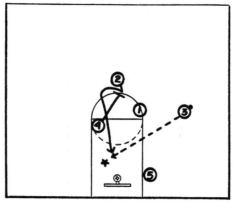

Diagram 7-19

The Portland Option

This option is very similar to the basic play of the Portland Trailblazers. When (2) receives the pass from (1), (3) is already at the wing (Diagram 7-20). Player (1)'s position tells (2) to fake to (3), and (5) to move up and screen for (3). Player (3) then cuts to the basket, looking for a lob pass from (2). See Diagram 7-21.

When player (5) sets the screen for (3), he tries to force a switch between X5 and X3. After (3) cuts and does not receive a lob pass from (2), he clears around the double screen of (1) and (4); (5) then rolls inside for a one-on-one play against the smaller X3. See Diagram 7-22.

Player (2) can pass to (5) inside, or to (3) around the double screen. When he passes to one of them, he screens away for the other. See the pass to (5) in Diagram 7-23 and the pass to (3) in Diagram 7-24.

The pass and screen away provides motion, an extra option, and keeps the defender busy to prevent a deep sag.

THE FULL-COURT OUT-OF-BOUNDS PLAYS FROM THE BACKCOURT BASELINE

The Horizontal Lineup

The opposition is playing a full-court man-to-man defense and denying the inbounds pass. The offense lines up with player (3) taking the ball out; the two big men, (4) and (5),

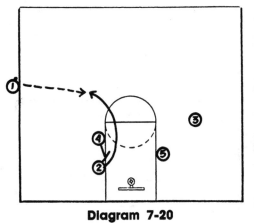

Diagram 7-20

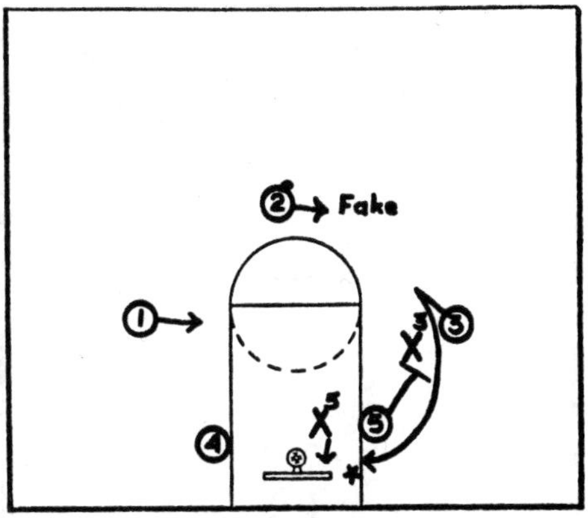

Diagram 7-21

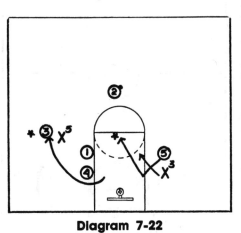

Diagram 7-22

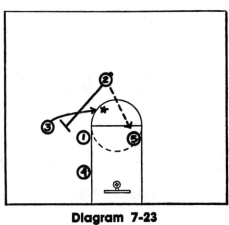

Diagram 7-23

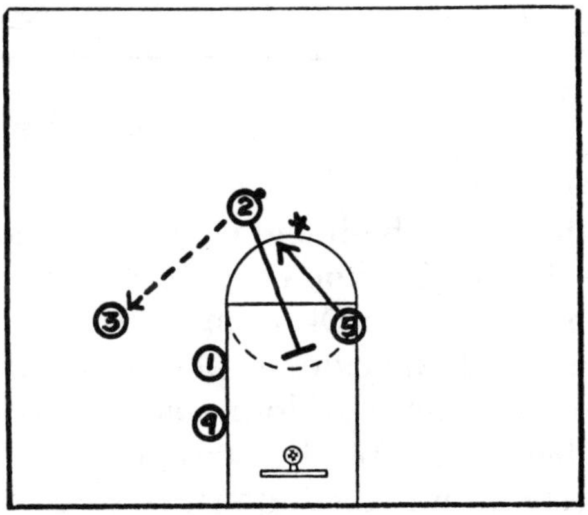

Diagram 7-24

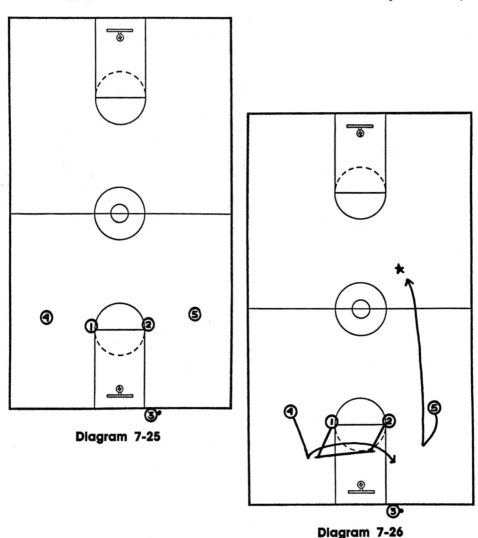

Diagram 7-25

Diagram 7-26

lineup free-throw-line high and close to the sidelines; and the two guards, (1) and (2), line up on each side of the lane and free-throw-line high. See Diagram 7-25.

Players (1) and (2) begin the play by screening for the off-side big man ((4)) who dips down and then comes to the ball. The onside big man ((5)) also starts toward the ball, but he changes direction and "flies" down court for a possible long pass. See Diagram 7-26.

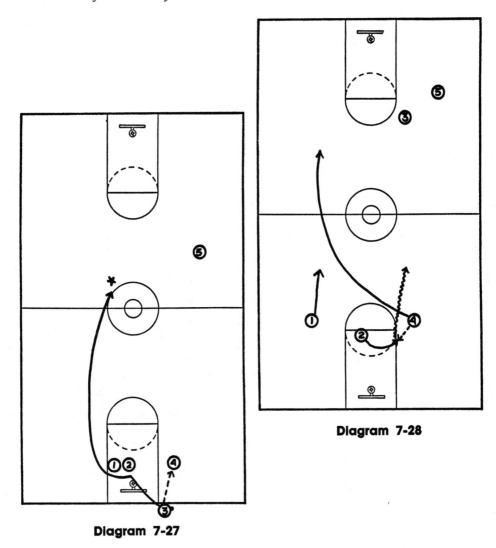

Diagram 7-28

Diagram 7-27

If player (3) passes to (4), his number one option, he ((3)) cuts off both guards as he "flies" downcourt (Diagram 7-27). If (4) cannot then pass to (3), he gives the ball to one of the guards to bring up-court. See Diagram 7-28.

If (3) cannot get the ball to (4), he passes to (2), who has moved around (1)'s downscreen. Player (3) then cuts off (4) and downcourt. If (3) is not open, players (1) and (2) bring the ball up-court. See Diagram 7-29.

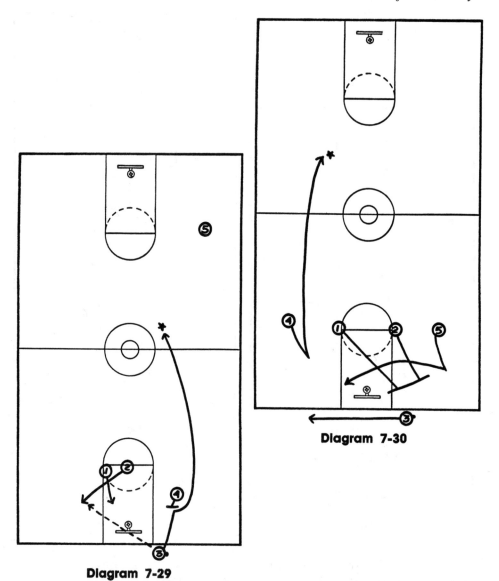

Diagram 7-30

Diagram 7-29

When making the inbounds pass after a score, (3) can change the side of the initial screen away of (1) and (2) by running the baseline. See Diagram 7-30.

This inbounds play also works versus zone presses because the initial alignment makes it impossible for them to cover from sideline to sideline.

BACKCOURT SIDELINE OUT-OF-BOUNDS PLAYS

Midcourt Lineup

As (3) takes the ball out at the backcourt sidelines, his teammates form a line at midcourt. Player (4) initiates the action by looping over the top of (1) and (2), and cutting to the basket. If this pass is not thrown, (4) clears to the offside. See Diagram 7-31.

Player (1) then cuts off (2) to the backcourt and receives a pass from (3); (3) cuts off (5) and looks for a return pass from (1). See Diagram 7-32.

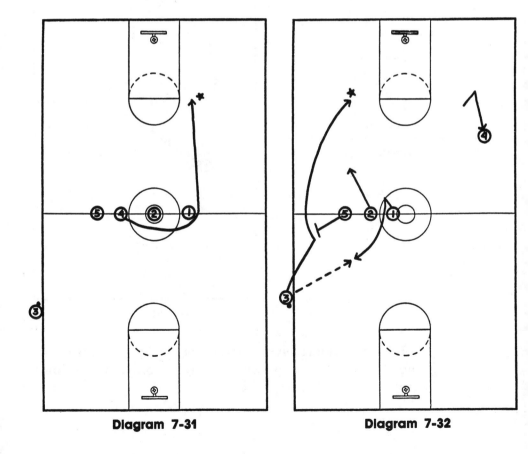

Diagram 7-31   Diagram 7-32

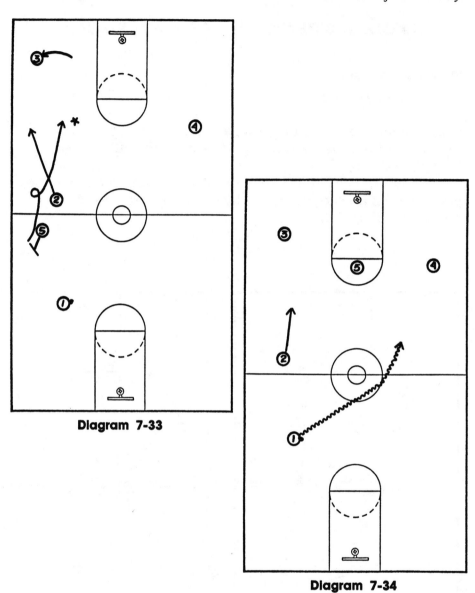

Diagram 7-33

Diagram 7-34

If (3) does not receive a pass from (1), player (2) moves opposite (1) and (5) uses him for a natural screen and cuts down
the middle. See Diagram 7-33.

If nothing develops, guards (1) and (2) bring the ball up-court and the team is in position to run their high-post offense. See Diagram 7-34.

These out-of-bounds plays provide a safe pass inbounds and several scoring options. Many of them may be used against either man-to-man or zone defenses.

The Hybrid Man-to-Man Defense

eight

There are two widely accepted approaches to man-to-man defense. They are:

A. One that emphasizes pass-denying pressure, lacks on-side help on the ball, makes ball reversal difficult, and expects most of the help to come from an offside defensive rotation. This defense was made famous by Dean Smith's North Carolina teams.

B. The Bobby Knight defense that provides much onside help on the ball, lacks some pass-denying function (especially ball reversal), and also expects help from an offside defensive rotation.

DEFENSIVE THEORY

In the final analysis, both of these defenses are made possible by the simple fact that offensive teams cannot put five men on the ball-side of the court and expect to have enough room to work. Because of this, most teams run offenses that consist of three-man plays (sometimes two-man plays). This leaves at least two offensive players away from the ball with little scoring potential. Today's defenses take advantage of this by playing tough defense on the ball, and what is, in effect, a zone on the offside. This offside zone rotates to the ball-side when any offensive penetration is threatened. As a result, the offense is playing three players against five defenders. There are three onside pressure players and two offside helpers.

The following approach to man-to-man defense borrows from both of these methods, adds a few ideas, and provides a viable team defense. It utilizes a four-man defensive perimeter and does not anticipate any help from the onside-post defender.

INDIVIDUAL DEFENSE

Defense on the Ball

For many years, the method of guarding the man with the ball was to stay between him and the basket and react to his movement. As the offensive players became more and more skilled, this was no longer effective. As, in most sports, the actor usually beats the reactor, this necessitated new defensive team techniques. Once methods of providing help from the offside were provided, the defensive man on the ball was able to become more aggressive and attack the ball. To play with this intensity, he had to have a stance that offered balance and mobility. The following defensive stance and rules have evolved:

When your man receives the ball, you "close out on him" by approaching with your weight on your back foot and your center of gravity down low.

1. Your feet are as wide as your shoulders.
2. Your inside foot is forward. This may make you more vulnerable to the middle, but that is where most of the help is located.
3. You are close enough to your opponent's knees to touch him.
4. You bend at the knees to lower your center of gravity. A good rule of thumb is to bend until the backs of your hands touch your kneecaps. This is a comfortable depth for most players. Be careful not to hunch your back or to bend at the waist.

5. Your palms are up, and the outside arm is the lead arm. It is used to trace the movement of the ball and attempt deflections. The inside arm is low and ready to contest a crossover dribble back to the middle.

6. Your eyes are fixed on your opponent's belt buckle.

7. You are prepared to play defense in a "step-step" manner while harassing the offensive man by swinging up at the ball with your lead hand.

8. If the offensive player picks up his dribble, you immediately grow tall by raising your center of gravity and attempting to get both hands on the ball. You inform your teammates that the man with the ball has picked up his dribble, and is in this predicament, by an oral signal such as "stick."

If you have done your job well, you have prevented him from entering the free throw lane, made him pick up his dribble, and your teammates are denying any pass to their man. After he passes the ball, you should jump toward the ball and make sure that any cut your man makes is not between you and the ball. We tell the players "never allow your man to cut by your face, and to the ball."

Defense Off the Ball

When your man does *not* have the ball, you should:

1. Open up and always see the ball.

2. Keep your shoulders parallel to the baseline with your nearest hand in the passing lane.

3. Be prepared to rotate on any penetration.

4. Do not be surprised by a crosscourt pass. Your job is to help *and* to recover.

5. Deny your man any "flash cut" to the ball. Be prepared to "plug" this cut to the ball in the same manner you block out for a rebound. See X4's "plug" in Diagram 8-1.

6. If you are the offside front man, you must be able to help inside and still be in position to recover and deny a

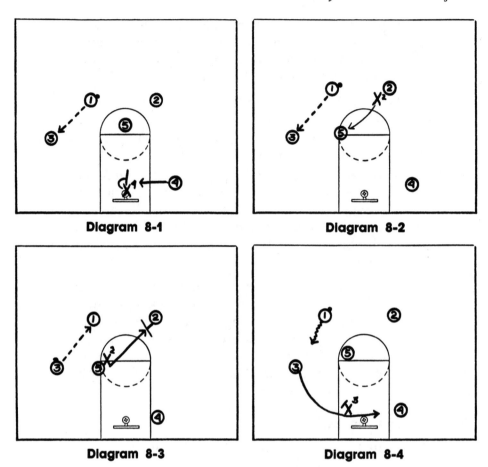

Diagram 8-1

Diagram 8-2

Diagram 8-3

Diagram 8-4

ball reversal. A good drill that demonstrates this technique is shown in Diagrams 8-2 and 8-3 (X2 helps on post man (5) and then recovers to deny the reversal by way of his man (2)).

7. If your man goes away from the basket to screen, you must "plug" the cutter and call the switch if one is necessary.

8. If your man clears across the lane to the offside, do not clear with him. Jam the lane. See defender X3 in Diagram 8-4.

9. Play no more than one step off the line of the ball to

your man. Playing there helps prevent backdoor plays and crosscourt lob passes.

10. Do not switch or double-team when helping. Your job is to help and then recover to your assigned man.

11. Remember that proper spacing should be maintained and that the rules are different once a penetration pass has been made.

TEAM DEFENSE VERSUS THE TWO-MAN FRONT

Phase I: Denying the Initial Penetration Pass and the Reversal Pass

As the opposition brings the ball up-court and before an initial penetration pass has been attempted, the Dean Smith Defense is preferable. To accomplish this defense, two simple rules are followed:

A. If you are one pass away from the ball, you deny any pass to your man by keeping your head between the ball and your man. Put your head on his numbers. See Players X2 and X3 in Diagram 8-5.

B. If you are two passes away, play in the lane with your shoulders parallel to the baseline. See X4 in Diagram 8-6.

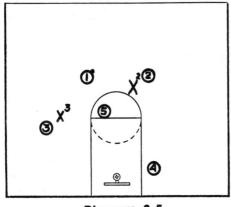

Diagram 8-5

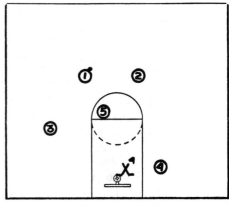

Diagram 8-6

Remember, this defense consists of a four-man perimeter and expects no help from the defensive post man (X5). His job is to front and deny the offensive post man (5).

Much practice time must be devoted both to a denial of the initial penetration pass and also any attempt to reverse the ball to the other side. It might be wise to make a team rule to the effect that if a defensive inside man permits two consecutive penetration passes to his man, or a guard allows the ball to be reversed two consecutive times by way of the man he is guarding, that player will come out of the game. At the very least, statistics should be kept that show who gave up penetration or reversal passes. For a given game, a review of the scouting report may offer clues to your defenders as to how the opposition initiates their offense. This report may also include their pressure-relieving devices that are designed to overcome the defensive denial attempt. Some examples would be:

1. the ball-side dribble entry
2. the diagonal dribble entry
3. clearouts
4. crossing the forwards
5. backdoor plays

Each should be discussed and plans should be made that permit the defenders to anticipate and defeat them. Practice time should be devoted to drills that feature repetitive practice of the proper defensive reaction to each of the offensive pressure-relieving devices. Some examples of proper responses would be as follows.

The Ball-side Dribble Entry

In Diagram 8-7, player (1) cannot make an entry pass so he chooses to key a play with a dribble entry. Two ways to defense this play are: a single-jump switch, and the run-and jump-defense.

A Single-Jump Switch: As Player (1) penetrates on the dribble, X3 steps out and jump switches with X1. This switch denies (1) much penetration and is possible because the offside help of X4 prevents (3) from cutting to the basket for an easy lay-up before X1 can get to him. Since player (1) was unable to make

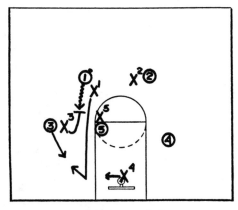

Diagram 8-7

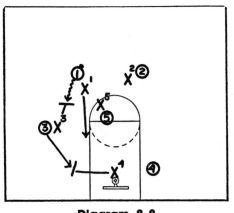

Diagram 8-8

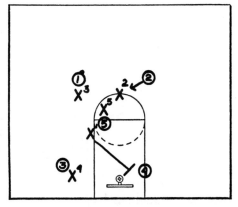

Diagram 8-9

much penetration, the play has been disrupted to a great extent. See Diagram 8-7.

Run-And-Jump Defense: If a run-and-jump defense were being used, X4 would be more active and actually step out on (3). Player X1 would then have the assignment of taking X4's man (Diagrams 8-8 and 8-9). Player (1) would then have the ball with no dribble left and have great difficulty making his next pass.

The Diagonal Dribble Entry

This play is being used quite often to combat ball-side pressure. The Diagonal Dribble Entry occurs when (1) cannot make the initial entry pass. Seeing (1)'s predicament, player (2)

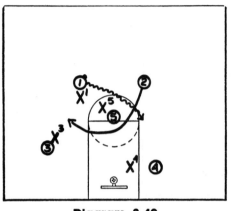

Diagram 8-10

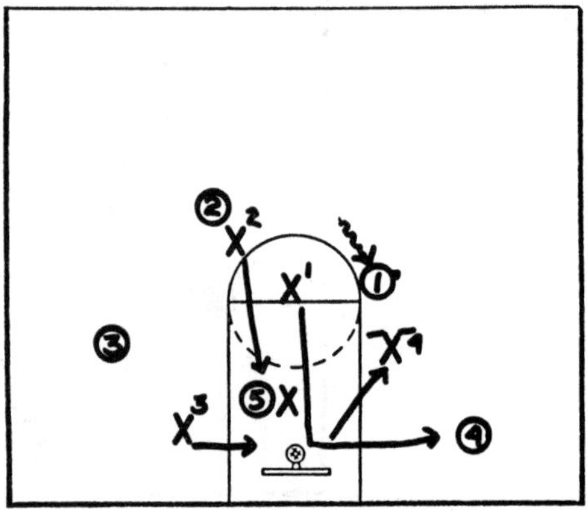

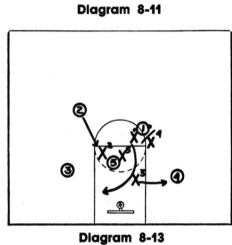

Diagram 8-11

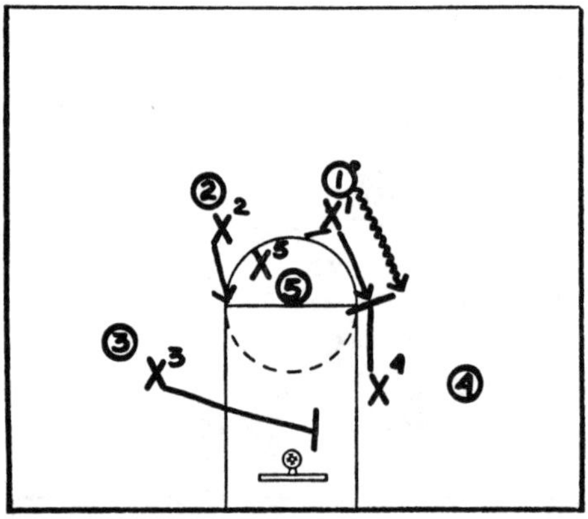

Diagram 8-12

Diagram 8-13

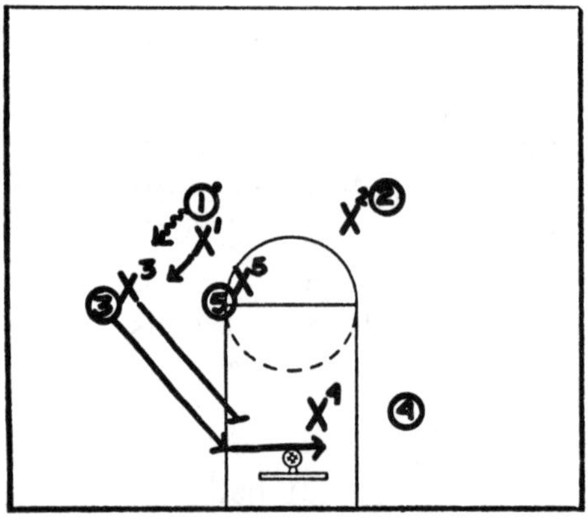

Diagram 8-14

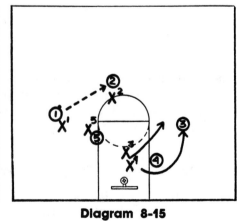

Diagram 8-15

clears down and around the high-post man, and (1) attempts to penetrate on a diagonal dribble. See Diagram 8-10.

The forward on the penetration side (X4) must step out and deny the diagonal dribble. The single-jump switch may be used (Diagram 8-11) or a run-and-jump sequence may be initiated. See Diagrams 8-12 and 8-13.

Forward Clearout

In Diagram 8-14, player (1) cannot make an entry pass and still has his dribble. Player (1)'s inability to pass tells forward (3) to clear out, and (1) to make a dribble entry. However, X3 follows his rule and does not clear across the lane from the ball-side; his refusal to clear across the lane jams the ball-side-post area and makes any potential post play difficult, if not impossible. Defender X3 must help and still be alert enough to get back to (3) if the ball is reversed to him. See Diagram 8-15.

Crossing the Forwards

This defensive play is a very popular pressure-relieving device and is usually keyed when the guards ((1) and (2)) cross as in Diagram 8-16.

Note that X3 again follows his rule and does not clear away from the ball-side. This refusal to clear away facilitates his switch with X4 and again leaves (2) with no initial pass. Note that X1 and X2 switched. Their switch allowed X1 to force (2) to pick up his dribble. See Diagram 8-17.

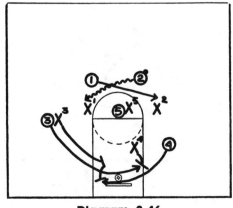

Diagram 8-16

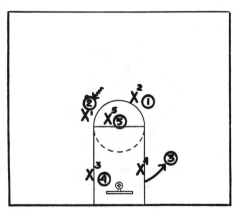

Diagram 8-17

Backdoor Plays

The Onside Backdoor Play. This play occurs when (3), after being denied by X3, goes behind him and looks for a bounce pass and a lay-up shot. The offside help as shown by X4 in Diagram 8-18 must come to the backdoor man and steal the ball, draw a step-in foul, or at least pick him up. The offside front man must drop down and assist the helper (X4) by taking (4).

The Offside Backdoor Play. In Diagram 8-19, (1) bounce passes to (4) cutting to the high-post area; (2) then backdoors his man. This play should be stopped by X4 who must beat (4) to the spot where the pass is received and deny the pass that keys the play. Defender X4 is taught that although he is the offside deep man and primary helper, he must always (when two passes away) play one step off a line from the ball to his man, and one-half of the way to the ball. This positioning permits him to beat (4) to the ball and still be able to rotate on any penetration.

These pressure-relieving plays are only a few examples of the many ways teams combat defensive pressure. However, the point being made is that it is possible to scout your opponent, be aware of their play-initiating and pressure-relieving techniques, make plans to counteract them, and through diligent practice, accomplish your goal.

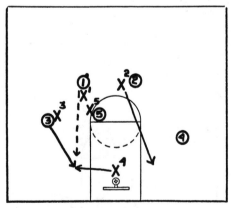

Diagram 8-18

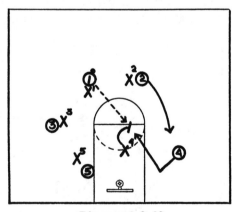

Diagram 8-19

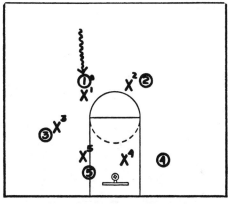

Diagram 8-20

Phase I of the defense has two basic strengths:

A. This phase makes it very difficult to make the initial entry pass that usually keys the offensive play.

B. The fact that the offside front defender plays tough pressure defense with his head between the ball and his man makes it difficult for the offense to reverse the ball to the weak side. See Diagram 8-20.

Phase II: Post-Penetration Pass Help and Recovery

Once the initial penetration pass is made, it is advantageous to utilize the Bobby Knight concepts because they create much pressure on the ball-side. The constant help-and-recover harassment makes it very difficult for the man with the ball to be creative. In Diagrams 8-21 and 8-22 player X1 sees that (3) is attempting to drive by X3 and makes a help-and-recover move that crowds (3) and forces him to pick up his dribble; X1 then recovers to pick up (1).

Player (3) then passes to Player (2) coming toward him and X3 executes the help-and-recover move. See Diagrams 8-23 and 8-24.

The constant ball-side-helping pressure of the Phase II defense is protected by offside deep man X4 in Diagram 8-24 who

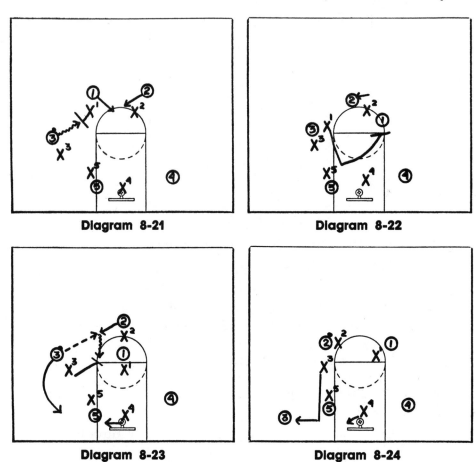

Diagram 8-21   **Diagram 8-22**

Diagram 8-23   **Diagram 8-24**

has sagged into the lane from the weak side. This onside pressure is the heart of the Indiana defense.

The Reset Play

It is very important, when the ball comes back out front after being entered, for the defensive quarterback to call out "one!" His call tells the defenders to return to Phase I which makes it difficult for the opposition to make a penetration pass or reverse the ball to the weak-side.

Functional Triangles

The functional triangles, formed by each helping defender playing one step off a line from the ball to his man, offer

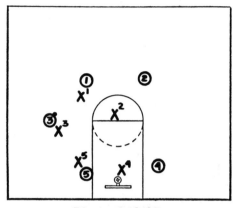

Diagram 8-25

assurance to the defender on the ball by placing the offside deep and front men one-half the way to the ball and in an open stance. This spacing permits him to be aware of, and have time to stop, ball-side penetration (X4 and X2 in Diagram 8-25). The onside helpers, by also playing one step off the line and, in their case, one-third off the way to the ball, may help and still recover to pick up their assigned man.

This positioning allows X3 to play tight on (3) and force him to make a hasty decision.

TEAM DEFENSE VERSUS A ONE-MAN-FRONT OFFENSE

When the offense utilizes a one-man front, the key is to turn the offense by overplaying the single point man. Overplaying the single point man dictates to the defenders which side will pressure and which side will be the help side. In Diagram 8-26, defender X1 forces (1) (the point man of the 1-4 offense) toward (2)'s side of the court. This force tells X2 to play pressure and deny any pass to (2), X4 to front the onside-post man (4), X5 that he is the offside deep, or primary, helper, and X3 that he must loosen up and be prepared to help the primary helper X5 if penetration occurs.

If X1 had forced the ball to (3)'s side:

1. X3 would deny any pass to (3).

2. X5 would then be guarding the post man and must front him.

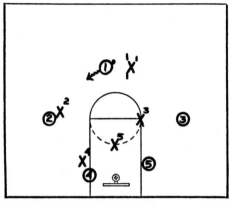

Diagram 8-26

3. X4 would be the offside deep man and thus the primary helper.

4. X2 would be the offside front man and will help the primary helper.

See Diagram 8-27.

From there, the rules would be the same with Phase I being used until a penetration pass is made which would key a switch to Phase II.

The combination of these two defensive theories assures that:

1. There will always be a great deal of pressure on the initial penetration pass.

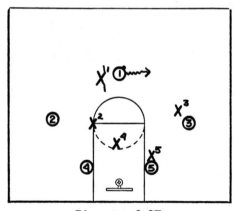

Diagram 8-27

2. It will be very difficult to enter the ball on one side and then reverse it to the other.

3. There will always be help-and-recover pressure on the ball-side.

4. Proper offside depth and distance will be maintained via the triangles.

5. Offside rotation and help will support the ball-side from the weak side.

In general, the team defense will profit from using the attributes, and eliminating the weaknesses, of the two leading defensive theories.

Zoning with Man-to-Man Principles

nine

Much has been written about playing man-to-man defense with zone principles. Theoretically, this concept permits you to adopt the strengths of both man-to-man and zone within the same defense. I feel these positive results may also be attained by playing a zone defense and utilizing man-to-man principles; the following two defenses do just that. The first defense uses the principles made popular by Bobby Knight. These principles include utilizing triangles and attempting to get help on both the offside and ball-side. The second defense gets more pressure on the initial penetration pass by the rule "one pass away equals pressure and two passes away equal help." This defense is an offshoot of the man-to-man defense rules that are attributed to Dean Smith.

THE BOBBY KNIGHT ZONE

Knowing Coach Knight's attitude toward zone defenses makes the title of this zone almost funny. However, I feel a very functional active perimeter-pressure zone may be developed using his man-to-man concepts.

161

The Initial Match-Up

The match-up device that best fits this zone would be my monster-plus-one concept. This matching method is initiated from a box-and-one. Players (1), (2), (3), and (4) form the box and big man (5) plays man-to-man on the ball-side-post man. See Diagram 9-1.

The "Bobby Knight" Zone Versus a Two-Man Front

If the offense comes up in a two-man front, the defense stays in the box-and-one shape and matches the offense. See Diagram 9-2.

The "Bobby Knight" Zone Versus a One-Man Front

If the offense comes up-court in a one-man front, the largest front man, X1 in Diagram 9-3, releases and covers both corners. This converts the box-and-one defense to a diamond-and-one. See Diagrams 9-3 and 9-4.

The "Bobby Knight" Zone
Versus a Two-Man Changing to a One-Man Front

If the offense comes up-court with a two-man front and then cuts a guard through (as many teams do), the front man on that side goes through with the cutter, calls out "one" to tell the other front man he went through, and then covers both corners. See X1 in Diagrams 9-5 and 9-6.

It must be remembered that in each of these situations, X5 is playing man-to-man on post man (5). This maneuver means, in man-to-man defensive parlance, that we intend to play pressure defense with a four-man rotating perimeter, and the defensive post man X5 will concentrate on the offensive post man (5).

UTILIZING THE MAN-TO-MAN PRINCIPLES

Turning the Offense

Once the initial match-up has been made, the Indiana man-to-man principles may be applied. The first (and one of the most important) man-to-man rules to be used is that the

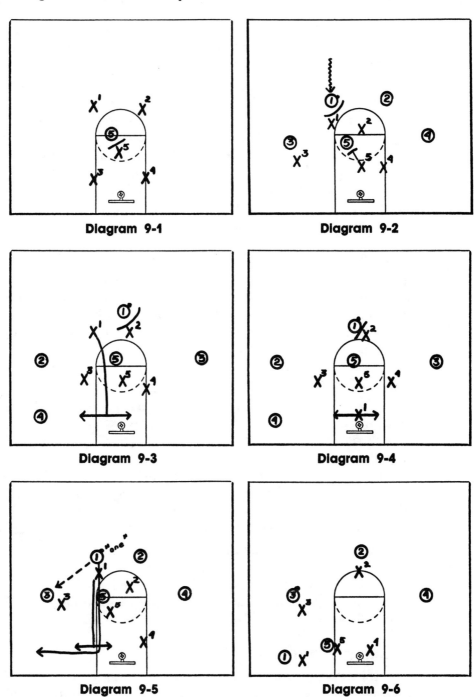

Diagram 9-1

Diagram 9-2

Diagram 9-3

Diagram 9-4

Diagram 9-5

Diagram 9-6

ball-side guard must play up on the ball and turn it to the out-side. See X1 versus a two-man front in Diagram 9-7, and versus a one-man front in Diagram 9-8.

Functional Triangles

Overplay by the ball-side front man declares the help-and-pressure side for the other zone players, and allows the team to play pressure on the ball-side and help on the offside. The positions the defenders assume are determined by following the triangle rule. In Diagram 9-9, players X2, X3, and X4 each become the apex of a triangle, the base of which is formed by a line from the ball to the man in their area.

Spacing

Note that players X2, X4, and X3 are one-third of the way to the ball and one step off the base of the triangle. Defender X5 is playing man-to-man. The turning of the ball by X1 and the help positions of the other players permit X3 and X5 to deny the entry pass that initiates plays.

Guard Cutters

If an entry pass is completed and a guard cuts through the front man, the defender on that side (X1 or X2) goes through with the cutter, calls out "one" to warn the other front man, and then covers both corners. This maneuver adjusts the zone to a diamond-and-one. The man-to-man rules are then followed from the resulting formation. See Diagrams 9-10 and 9-11.

Penetration Equals Rotation

An example of the man-to-man rules being followed would occur if X3's denial position allowed (3) to penetrate after receiving the pass from (1). The offside help, X4 and X2, would make a rotation that would permit them to help on (3) until X3 recovered. See Diagrams 9-12 and 9-13.

Functional Stances

It is very important when playing the "Bobby Knight" type of zone that the offside help assume good man-to-man-help

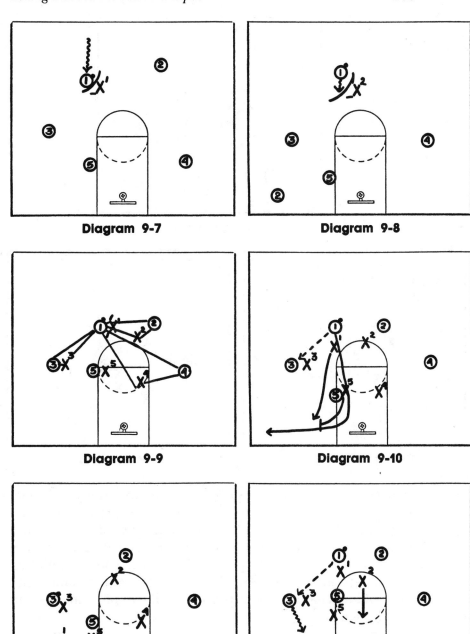

Diagram 9-7

Diagram 9-8

Diagram 9-9

Diagram 9-10

Diagram 9-11

Diagram 9-12

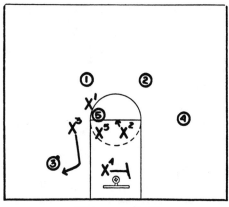

Diagram 9-13

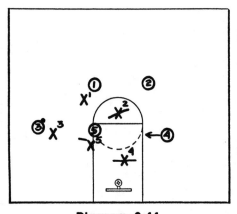

Diagram 9-14

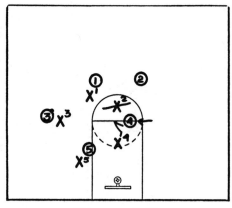

Diagram 9-15

stances, rather than the usual straight up-and-down ball-side-facing zone stances. The defenders must open up and be in position to see the man in their area and the ball. This stance makes it possible for them to help and recover quickly and also permits them to see and "plug" offside cutters to the ball. Diagrams 9-14 and 9-15 show X4 assuming a proper stance with his shoulders parallel to the baseline and then plugging (4)'s cut to the high post.

Help and Recover

It should be pointed out that the strength of this defensive concept is that it provides help on the ball-side as well as the

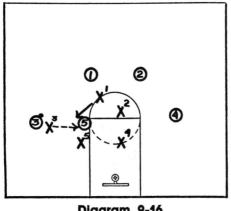

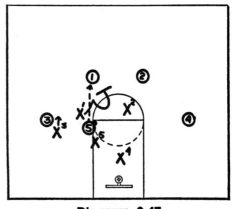

| Diagram 9-16 | Diagram 9-17 |

offside. The defenders are taught that they must fall off and help on the ball-side and still be able to recover to pick up the man in their area. In Diagrams 9-16 and 9-17, player X1 helps on the post man, but still recovers to cover a return pass to the man in his area.

The Penetration Dribble

One of the banes of coaching zone defense is the penetration dribble. This defensive plan handles that problem more efficiently than most zones. Two examples are as follows:

A. Baseline-Side Guard Penetration

In Diagrams 9-18 and 9-19, guard (1) gets by defender X1 to the baseline side. Defender X3 helps by stopping (1)'s dribble until X1 can get there; X3 then recovers to defend (3) in his area.

Note in Diagrams 9-18 and 9-19 that X4 and X1 started their offside rotation as (1) began to penetrate from the side away from them.

B. Guard Penetration Down the Middle

In Diagram 9-20, Player (1) penetrates inside of defender X1 and is picked up by defender X2.

X2 then must recover to defend (2) when a pass is made to him. See Diagram 9-21.

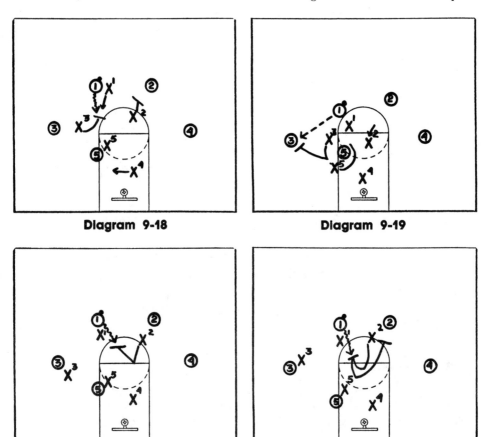

Diagram 9-18   Diagram 9-19

Diagram 9-20   Diagram 9-21

Wing Cutters

Players X3 and X4 are always defensive wing men. If the offense is in a two-man front, they are the back-wing men of what is, in effect, a 2-3 zone. See Diagram 9-22.

When the offense is in a one-man front, defenders X3 and X4 are the wing men of what is, in effect, a 1-3-1 zone (Diagram 9-23). Their rules versus cutters regardless of the formation are much like the man-to-man practice. They never let the cutter "go across their face." This means they do not allow him to cut between them and the ball. They follow him for two steps and then look for the "release" man. The release man is the man who will come into their zone to replace the cutter. In Diagram

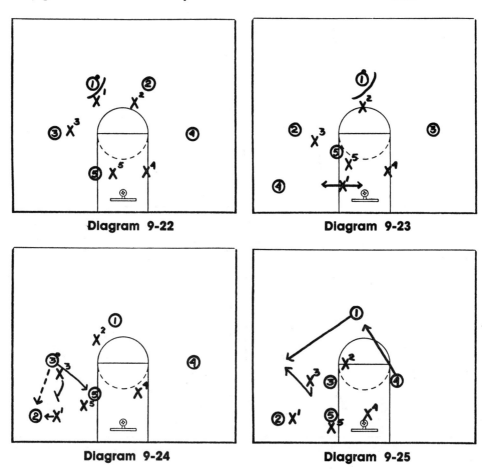

Diagram 9-22   Diagram 9-23

Diagram 9-24   Diagram 9-25

9-24, offensive player (3) passes to (2) in the corner and cuts through.

X3 does not allow (3) to cut across his face and then falls off to pick up release man (1), who is coming into his zone. If possible, he denies (2)'s pass to (1). See Diagram 9-25.

Note that the offside helper X4 was ready to rotate across and help if needed.

Second Cutters from the Front

We have covered the initial match-up. This included a cutting situation for the front men. (The rule was: When the offense sent a guard through, the guard on that side went

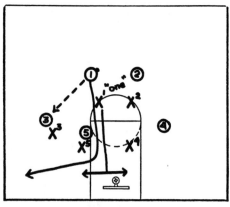

Diagram 9-26

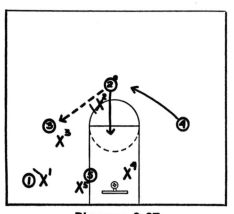

Diagram 9-27

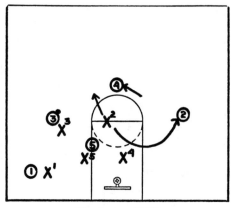

Diagram 9-28

through with him and called out "one" to tell the remaining front man we were in a one-man-front zone, and he was the lone front man.) Once this has been done, the lone front man uses the same rule as the wing man. For example, in Diagram 9-26, player (1) cuts through and X1 goes with him; X1 calls out "one."

Player X2 now knows he is the lone front man. In Diagrams 9-27 and 9-28, (2) then cuts through. Defender X2 knows he should not allow (2) to cut across his face. X2 follows him through for two steps, and picks up the release man (4).

Covering a Pass to the Post

When a pass is made to the post using the monster-and-one defense, that pass is usually well-covered. Defender X5 plays man-to-man on the post man (5) and the others sag in to help. See Diagram 9-29, Pass to Post versus a One-Man Front and Diagram 9-30, Pass to Post versus a Two-Man Front.

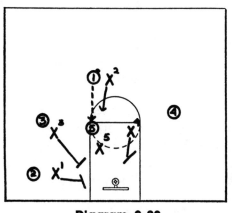

Diagram 9-29

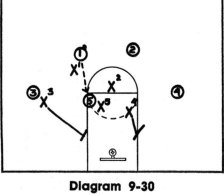

Diagram 9-30

Note that players X3 and X4 always pinch to their respective lay-up slots.

By playing this zone with man-to-man concepts, we can: Put more pressure on the initial penetration pass, use help-and-recover techniques, play the post man man-to-man, assure that we have offside help, improve our offside zone fundamentals, and, in general, develop a more active zone defense.

THE DEAN SMITH ZONE WITH MAN-TO-MAN PRINCIPLES

Initial Match-up

This zone would make its initial match-up from a 2-3 set. It is a five-man zone; X5 does not play man-to-man.

If the offense came up the court in a two-man front set, the defense would not need to adjust.

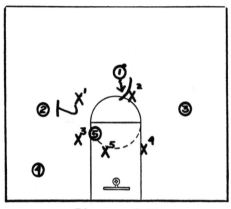

Diagram 9-31

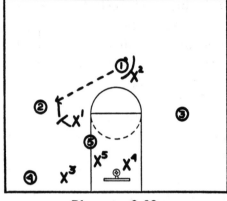

Diagram 9-32

If the offense came up-court in a one-man front set, the smaller front man X2 would take the point and the larger one X1 a side man. See Diagrams 9-31 and 9-32.

As shown in Diagram 9-32, X2 would then attempt to turn (1) toward X1; X1 would be in good position to deny (2).

Front Cutters Versus a Two-Man Front

When the offense came up in a two-man front and a guard, (1) in Diagram 9-33, cut through, the front man on that side, X1, would go through with him. He, X1, would not let (1) cut across his face. Player X1 would then go through and cover the next man away from the ball from X2. See Diagram 9-34.

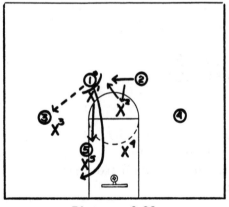

Diagram 9-33

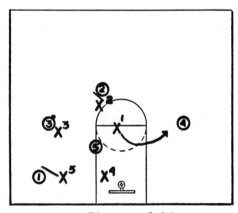

Diagram 9-34

From there, X1 uses the same rules he used versus a one-man front.

The Rules in Action Versus a Two-Man Front

After this initial match-up, Dean Smith's man-to-man rules, with a few exceptions, would be used. The basic rule is "one pass away equals pressure and two passes away equal help." See these rules in action versus an even-man front in Diagrams 9-35 through 9-39.

Ball in Front

In Diagram 9-35, the players are shown in the positions they would assume when the ball is out front. Defender X1 is tight on the ball, X2 and X3 are one pass away so they play pressure, and X4 is two passes away and plays in the lane.

Ball on Side

Diagram 9-36 shows the 2-3 positions when the ball is on the side with X3 tight on the ball, X5 and X1 playing pressure, X2 in the lane, and X4 denying the onside post man.

Side to Corner Pass

Once the ball goes to the corner, John Egli's sliding 2-3 zone rules would be in effect, and X3 would slide in between X5 and X4. See Diagram 9-37.

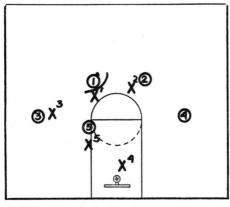

Diagram 9-35
Ball in Front

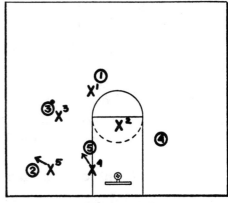

Diagram 9-36
Ball on Side

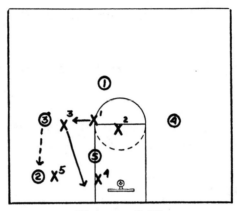

Diagram 9-37
Side to Corner Pass

Out of Corner Passes

Player X1 would then move out to the side and take the next two passes out of the corner. See Diagrams 9-38 and 9-39.

This move put the team back in a 2-3 zone and X5 and X3 interchanged positions. Note that X2 protected the lane as X1 took the two passes out of the corner.

The Rules in Action Versus a One-Man Front

When the offense comes up in a one-man front, the defense tilts toward X1's side. Defender X2 takes in the point and X1 takes the wing. Note that X2 forces the ball to X1's side. See Diagram 9-40.

The defense then has two distinct sides—the tilted side and the open side.

A. *The Tilted Side.* When the ball is passed to the tilted side, no special problems occur. See Diagrams 9-41 and 9-42.

B. *The Open Side.* When the ball is passed to the open side (away from the force), adjustments are made:

Front to Side Pass

In Diagram 9-43, player (1) passes to the open side which is the side opposite the force. This pass tells X4 to hustle and cover the wing.

Diagram 9-38

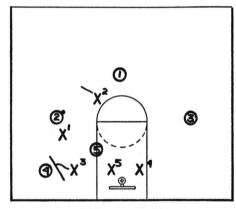

Diagram 9-39

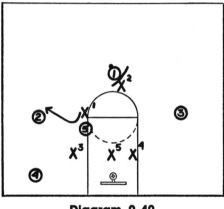

Diagram 9-40

Diagram 9-41
Ball on Side

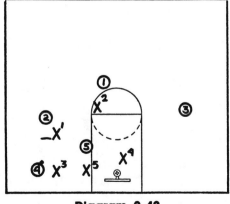

Diagram 9-42
Ball in Corner

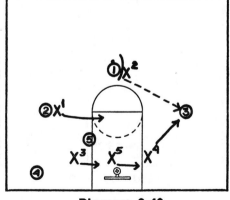

Diagram 9-43
Front to Side Pass

Side to Corner Pass

When the ball is passed to the corner, X5 must take it; X4 slides in between X5 and X3. See Diagram 9-44.

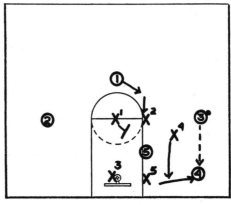

Diagram 9-44
Side to Corner Pass

Out of Corner Pass

Player X2 takes the next two passes out of the corner and the zone is back in the tilted 2-3 formation. See Diagrams 9-45 and 9-46.

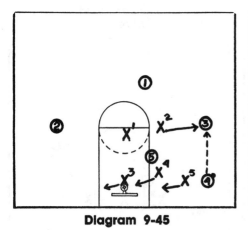

Diagram 9-45

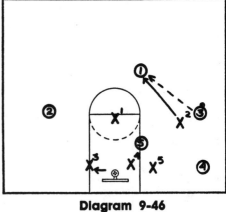

Diagram 9-46

Wing Cutters

This defense would use John Egli's rules in regard to wing cutters. When an offensive wing man passes to the corner and cuts through, the defensive wing man X3 cuts to the offside-rebound area. This rule makes X3, X5, and X4 interchangeable again. After this happens, the front man on that side, X1, must cover the next two passes out of the corner. See Diagrams 9-47 through 9-49.

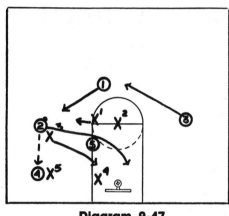

Diagram 9-47

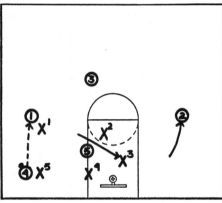

Diagram 9-48

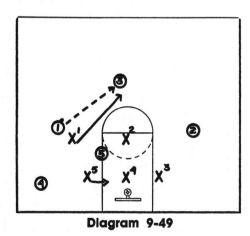

Diagram 9-49

X1's responsibility puts the zone back in a 2-3 shape and we are ready to use the same rules as the ball is moved around the perimeter.

Note that X1 taking two passes out of the corner violates the rule of "one pass away equals pressure and two passes away equal help," but we are not too interested in denying the ball's return to the front of the zone.

Covering a Pass to the Post

When the ball is passed to the high- or low-post man, all five defenders must jam the lane and help. Diagram 9-50 shows a pass to the post versus an odd front. The middle of the back

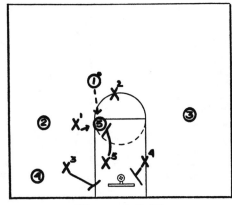

Diagram 9-50

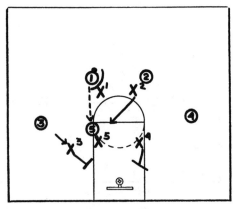

Diagram 9-51

three defenders (X5) takes the ball and X3 and X4 jam the lay-up slots.

Diagram 9-51 shows a pass to the post versus an even front. Middle man X5 again takes the ball and X3 and X4 jam the lay-up slots.

This zone may lack the ball-side-help ability of the Bobby Knight zone, but it allows for greater denial pressure on the ball-side. It encourages the defender to assume the stance and attitude of man-to-man defenders and results in a more functional zone defense.

Applying Zone Pressure

ten

The use of zone pressure has become a complicated strategy. Most teams have a "well-thought out" plan and have devoted much practice time to this phase of their offensive game. A great deal of material has been written, and fairly standard methods have been developed to beat the zone press. But the standardization of offensive techniques is a two-edged sword because it also permits the defensive zone-pressure coach to make certain assumptions that may increase the chances of success for his defense. Some of these are:

ZONE-PRESS ASSUMPTIONS ON THE INBOUNDS PASS

Most teams are right-handed and will take the ball out on that side as you face downcourt. These teams have also been taught not to take the ball out under their backboard, and that forces them farther to the right. These factors permit the defense to overshift their zone press to that side.

Many teams will attempt to blitz your press by taking the ball out quickly and throwing long. If you choose to invert your defense by taking the time to allow the big men to get back and the small men to get up front, someone must protect the basket until these two things occur. One defender must also quickly pressure the inbounds passer and a small man must protect that defender's zone temporarily until a big man gets back.

181

You must expect that some teams will either run the baseline after a score or make a pass behind the baseline. Your pressure zone must slide as if the ball were inbounds.

The most likely place for the inbounds pass to be received is on the right side and inside the backcourt free throw line. Put your best defenders on that side.

ZONE-PRESS ASSUMPTIONS ON THE PENETRATION PASS

Once the inbounds pass has been made, the offense usually plans to make a penetration pass to the middle of the press, followed by a reverse pass to the weak side. See Diagram 10-1.

Some teams will circumvent the pass to the middle and simply lob crosscourt to an open player moving up the weak side. These options are made possible because a strong zone-

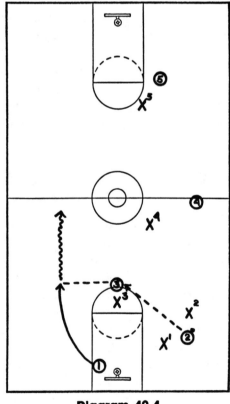

Diagram 10-1

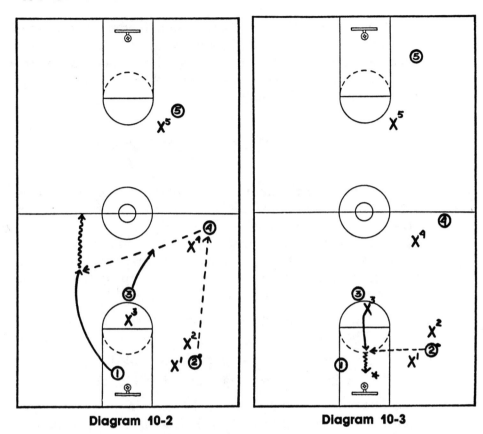

Diagram 10-2   **Diagram 10-3**

pressure defense will usually station all five of the defenders on the ball-side of the court. If the middle penetration or lob pass is not available, many teams will throw up the ball-side sideline and then pass to the middle, followed by a pass to the weak side. See Diagram 10-2.

Much time must be spent in practice, defensing these most-desired offensive options. Along with these options, teams may be forced into more dangerous maneuvers; they may even throw guard-to-guard passes across the free throw lane. Your team must be taught that their prime objective is to keep the ball out of the middle of the press, but that if this pass can be intercepted, an easy basket will follow. See X3 in Diagram 10-3.

The defenders should also be aware that offensive players, when double-teamed, may attempt to split the double team by dribbling between the defenders. One defender must stop the man with the ball and the other must seal the double-team by keeping his foot close to the "stopper." A discussion of the charging rule and how it is interpreted in your area is very much in order at this time.

ZONE-PRESS ASSUMPTIONS ON THE SCORING PLAY

The most pertinent question in regard to the scoring play is "Will they take the ball all the way to the basket whenever possible, or do they desire to beat the press and then set up their basic half-court offense?" This information should be in the scouting report for a given team, and may determine when the defense will retreat to their basic half-court defense. Some of the methods used to key the retreat are:

1. Stay in it until the defensive quarterback calls "zone." Then retreat to the lane and into the half-court defense.

2. Retreat after the first double-team in the frontcourt.

3. Stay in it until we steal the ball or they score.

The scouting report should also contain their basic alignment, and the strengths and weaknesses of their personnel.

The following zone-pressure defenses are designed around the preceding assumptions. The defenses included in this chapter are: A 3/4 press that on key can be a trapping zone or a run and jump defense; a defense that starts out man-to-man and becomes a trapping 1-3-1 zone once the opposition is in their man-to-man offense; a 1-2-1-1 full-court trapping zone press, designed to counter the newest innovation in zone press offense, which is the "trailing big man offense." The two methods are the single backcourt trap plan, and "the offside wing man up" plan.

A CHANGING THREE-QUARTER-COURT PRESS

This press relies on the element of surprise. It starts with the two defensive guards (X1 and X2) meeting the two offensive guards ((1) and (2)) at a point between the two backcourt

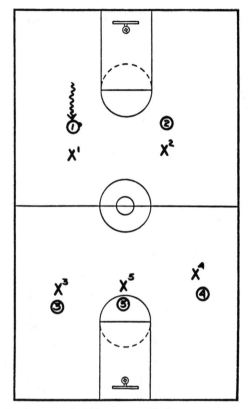

Diagram 10-4

circles, and the frontcourt defenders (X3, X4, and X5) fronting their men. See Diagram 10-4.

As defenders X1 and X2 meet the offensive guards, either of two options may be keyed:

    a. The defenders may force the guard with the ball to the inside and key a run and jump sequence.

    b. The defenders may force the guard with the ball down the side and key a double-teaming zone trap sequence.

The Run and Jump

The run-and-jump sequence is keyed when a defensive guard (X1 in Diagram 10-5) turns his man inside and forces him to dribble. When this happens, the offside guard (X2) jumps out and stops him.

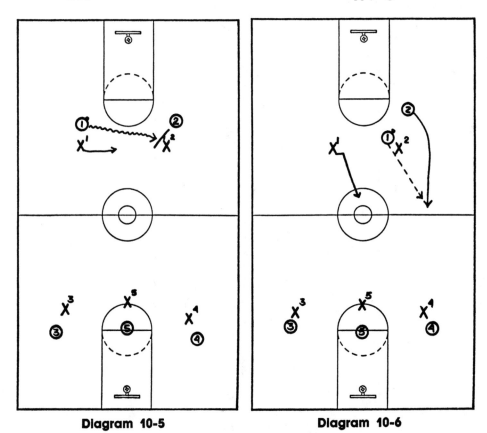

Diagram 10-5   **Diagram 10-6**

After X2 steps out, the natural tendency for the man he is guarding ((2)) is to cut down the sideline and toward the basket. X2's jump switch will usually cause (1) to pick up his dribble, and very often he will be forced to pass to (2). See Diagram 10-6.

Defender X4 anticipates (1)'s pass and may attempt to: intercept, draw a step-in foul, or stop (2)'s penetration abruptly after he catches the ball. To compensate for X4 leaving his man, the inside of the defense must rotate toward the ball. This can be done with the middle man X5 being part of the rotation. See Diagram 10-7.

The rotation may also be made in a four-man fashion with X5 staying in the middle. This forces X3, the offside forward, to make an extremely long rotation, but X5 can keep the ball

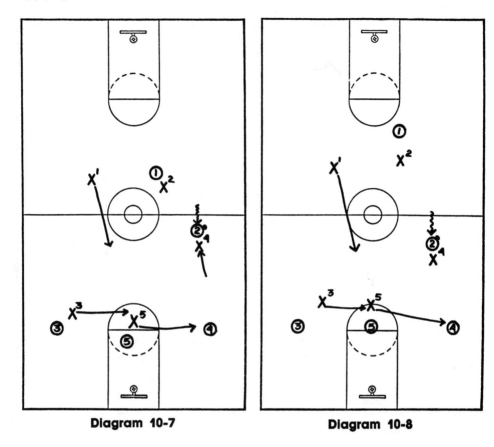

Diagram 10-7   **Diagram 10-8**

out of the middle, which is the Achilles' heel of the run-and-jump defense. See Diagram 10-8.

Note in the Diagram 10-8 above that X3 started his move as soon as X1 turned (1) to the inside. Player X5's rule is then to keep the ball out of the middle and beat the ball to the basket.

It should be noted that X1's rotation should be done facing the ball. Very often (2), upon receiving the pass from (1), will dribble to the middle. When this happens, X1 can jump-switch on him. See Diagrams 10-9 and 10-10.

Another play situation occurring often is when (2), after catching the pass from (1), passes to the open man on the ball-side wing. The man rotating to that area, either X3 or X5, must really hustle to get there.

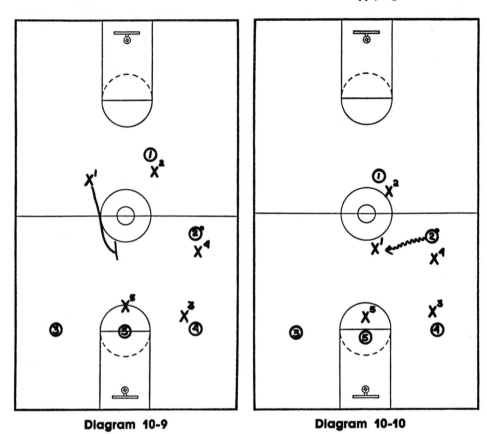

Diagram 10-9   **Diagram 10-10**

From that situation the run and jump consists of forcing the man with the ball to dribble, then jump-switching on him; the primary rule is "if you take my man, I must take yours." No double teams are desired.

The Zone Trap

In Diagram 10-11, defender X1 forces his offensive man to dribble down the side; his play keys the zone-trap double-teaming sequence. Player X3 moves up to stop the ball, X2 slides down to jam the middle, and X5 and X4 become the back men of the three-quarter-trap defense; X4 protects the basket while X5 covers the open ball-side wing.

The slides are the same as any half- or three-quarter-court press. See Diagrams 10-12 and 10-13.

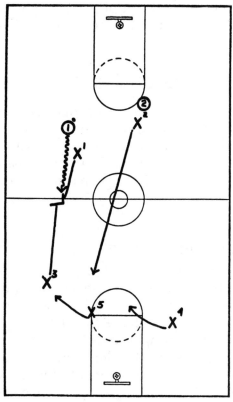

Diagram 10-11

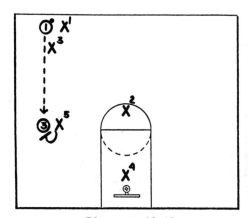

Diagram 10-12
Front to Side Press

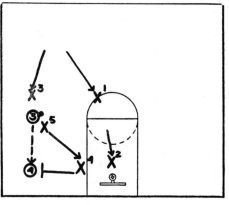

Diagram 10-13
Side to Corner Press

By varying the two types of presses, this plan adds an element of surprise and may confuse even a well-organized team.

THE DELAYED PRESS

Most teams have a plan to face zone pressure and feel they are ready to face it. If your defense shows zone press, and the opposition can read it, you may have a problem. This zone-pressure defense starts man-to-man and changes to a 1-3-1 trapping zone on key. The keys that may switch the defense are.

A Guard Dribble Reversal

When your defensive guard (X1 in Diagram 10-14) forces offensive guard (1) to reverse dribble toward the sideline, X1 stops him using the sideline and X2 double-teams him. This maneuver converts the defense to a 1-3-1 trapping zone and makes X1 the onside wing man, X2 the point man, X4 the offside wing man, and X3 the baseline roamer, who will cover both corners of the 1-3-1 trapping zone. Defender X5 will play between the ball and the basket and fill all the holes. See Diagram 10-15.

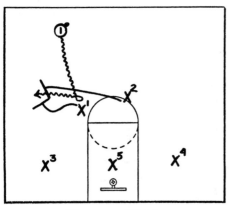

Diagram 10-14

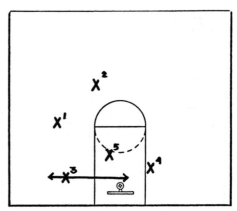

Diagram 10-15

A Pass to the Deep Corner

When a pass to the deep corner occurs, such as (1) passing to (3) (Diagram 10-16), the back man on that side stops the ball and the onside front man may come down to double-team it. This maneuver would convert the man-to-man defense into a 1-3-1 trapping zone with X1 becoming the onside wing man, X3 the baseline roamer, X2 the point man, X4 the offside wing man, and X5 staying between the ball and the basket. See Diagram 10-17.

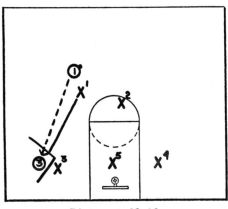

Diagram 10-16

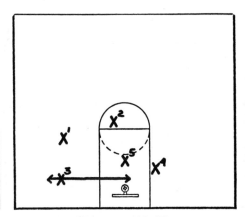

Diagram 10-17

The Third Pass

The usual and best method of keying the defensive change is to allow them to initiate their man-to-man offense, and then on the third pass double-team and convert to a 1-3-1 trapping zone. It may take some scouting to be able to anticipate their movement and execute this conversion. In Diagram 10-18, (1) makes the penetration pass to (3) and cuts through; defender X1 goes with him. Offensive player (3) then attempts to reverse the ball to (1) by way of (2) (Diagram 10-19). The pass to (2) is the second pass and the pass to (3) is the third. Defender X2 calls out "three" and double-teams (1). See Diagram 10-20.

Defender X2 is now the point man, X1 the ball-side wing man, X4 the baseline roamer, X3 the offside wing man, and X5 plays the middle of a 1-3-1 trapping zone. See Diagram 10-21.

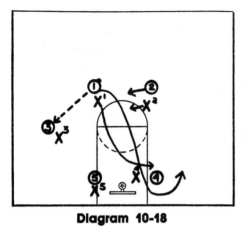

Diagram 10-18

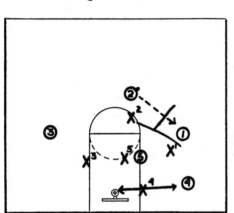

Diagram 10-20

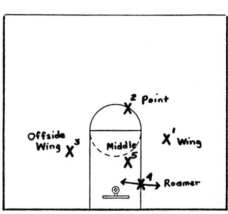

Diagram 10-21

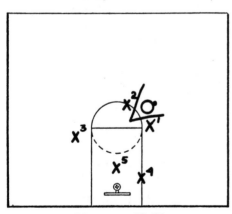

Diagram 10-22

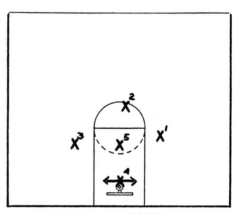

Diagram 10-23

It is wise when planning to use this delayed press to start the game playing man-to-man. Once the offense has settled into their man-to-man game, the defense can start trapping. A coach could say "We will play straight man-to-man until they score ten points, then we will run our delayed press." It is also wise to take the press off on occasions and then come back to it. When in doubt, remember that after the first trap, the onside front man, X1 in Diagram 10-22, becomes a wing man; the offside front man becomes the point man (X2); the offside deep man becomes the offside wing man (X3), onside deep man X4 becomes the baseline roamer; and the big middle man (X5) guards the post man, and plays the middle of the zone. See Diagrams 10-22 and 10-23.

The situations presented here are rather tailor-made, and the opposition's alignment won't always be so symmetric. However, as the season progress, your defenders will learn to scramble from a man-to-man defense to the 1-3-1 trapping zone on key. The mental pressure is actually on the offense because no one practices converting their man-to-man offense to a zone-trap offense.

DEFENSING THE TRAILING BIG MAN

The newest innovation in zone-press offense is the use of the trailing big man. In the past, reversing the ball against zone pressure involved a great deal of risk. The reversal was usually attempted in one of two ways: a pass to the middle of the press and a subsequent pass to the weak side (Diagram 10-24) or a lob pass to the weak side (Diagram 10-25).

When the lob pass was made, the pass demanded much skill because it was, and is, tough to time and judge; the pass resulted in many errors. The advent of the trailing big man makes it possible to reverse the ball with minimal risk. This reversal forces the defense to switch sides of the court, which, in turn, demands many changes in assignments and lateral movement.

Couple these demands with the fact that the trailing big man can make fakes before throwing to either side and the de-

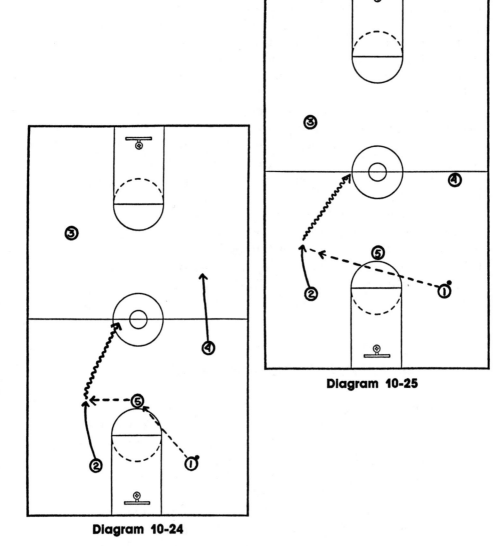

Diagram 10-25

Diagram 10-24

fensive assignments become virtually impossible. See Diagrams 10-26 and 10-27 which show a reversal utilizing the trailing big man ((3)) versus a 1-2-1-1 trapping zone.

The defenders are required to cover so much area on the quick reversal by way of the trailing big man ((3)), that very of-

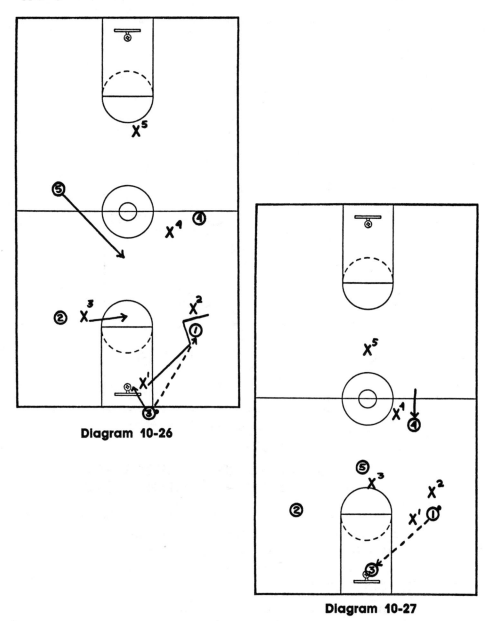

Diagram 10-26

Diagram 10-27

ten a hole is created in the middle of the zone. This hole can lead to a penetration pass and a subsequent pass to the weak side. See Diagram 10-28.

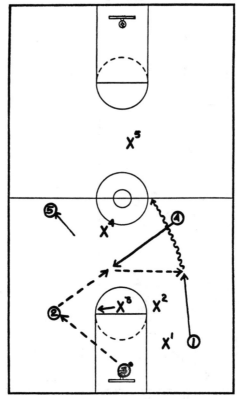

Diagram 10-28

1-2-1-1 DEFENSIVE ADJUSTMENTS
TO THE TRAILING-BIG-MAN OFFENSE

These new trailing-big-man offensive technique necessitates adjustments by the defense. Two examples of the adjustments a 1-2-1-1 pressure zone can make are as follows:

The Single Trap

In Diagram 10-29, X1, the point man of the 1-2-1-1 defense, does not pressure the inbounds pass. He sets up as high as the backcourt free throw line, and faces the strong side. Player X1's initial job is to deny any pass to the free throw lane area. Both wings, X2 and X3, deny the man on their side and

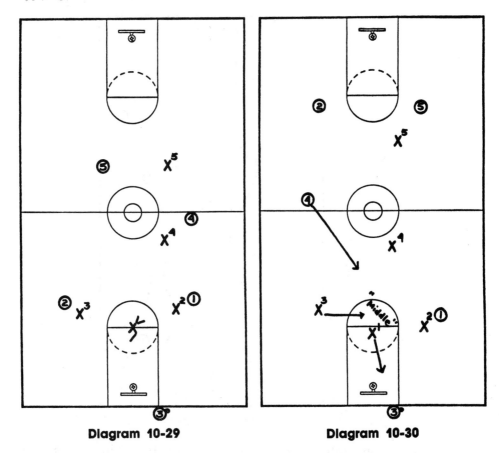

Diagram 10-29   **Diagram 10-30**

attempt to force the inbounds pass to be a high lob to the outside.

If there is no one on their side, they (X2 and X3) jam the middle, call out "Middle"; this signal tells X1 to initially take the inbound passer (3). See X3 in Diagram 10-30.

Once the ball comes inside, no matter what offensive alignment is used, X1 calls "ball" and takes (3) to deny any reverse. The offside wing man (X3 in Diagram 10-31) jams the middle and X4 hustles quickly to the ball-side. Defender X2 then runs the ball handler down the side. Player X4 stops the ball and X2 seals the double-team.

Note that X4 did not come to the ball; he waited and stopped it in his area. Also note that X3 came to the middle and

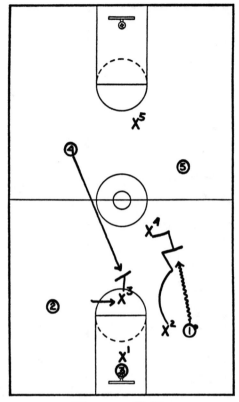

Diagram 10-31

stayed as high as the ball, and that X1 denied any reversal by way of the trailing big man ((3)). *This single trap defensive adjustment*:

1. Makes the inbounds pass difficult by denying any pass to the wings and placing X1 in the middle.

2. Negates the trailing-big-man reversal by having X1 cover him in a man-to-man fashion once the inbounds pass was made.

3. Causes the first double-team to occur at midcourt with X2 forcing (2) down the side and X4 stopping him.

4. Protects the middle with the offside wing man (X3 in Diagram 10-31) once the ball has been inbounded.

The Offside Wing Up

The second adjustment that can be made to the trailing-big-man maneuver is to have the offside wing man cover him after the inbounds pass. In Diagram 10-32, Player (3) passes to (1), who is quickly double-teamed by onside wing man X2 and point man X1. The offside wing man (X3), who was overshifted and stationed at the free throw line, moves up to take trailing big man (3). See Diagram 10-33.

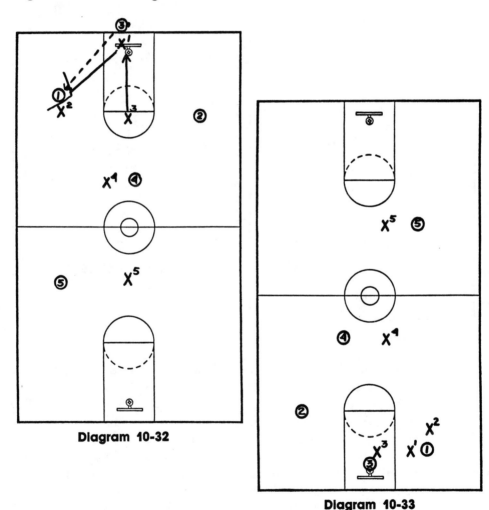

Diagram 10-32

Diagram 10-33

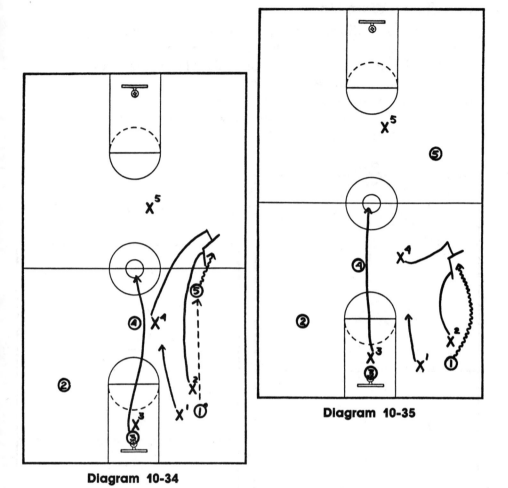

Diagram 10-35

Diagram 10-34

Defender X4 must stay in the middle until a penetration pass or penetration dribble is made; he then must run a difficult pursuit pattern to stop the ball. Once X4 stops it, X2, the onside wingman, will double-team the ball. See the pass penetration and defensive slides in Diagram 10-34.

Note that this penetration pass released X3 and gave him the difficult task of catching up with, and playing as high as the ball. The pass also released X1 to run for the basket.

In Diagram 10-35, player (1) dribbles down the side and the same rules prevail.

Index

Triangle cut, 49
Triangle featuring a 1-3-1 set with
    baseline roamer, 48
Triangle play, 46
Turning the offense, 162–64
Turnovers, 93
Two-hand overhead pass, 72
    double-teamed, 81
Two-man to one-man front, 162
2-2-1 UCLA press, 93

U

UCLA cut play, 2
UCLA entry play, 13
UCLA semistall, 108–12
    basic scoring option, 109–10
    personnel alignment, 108
    stall phase, 111–12
Utilizing fundamentals, 59
Utilizing triangles, 13

V

Variety, 59
Varying offensive perimeter, 36, 55
"V" cut, 24, 26
Vertical lineup series, 129–33
    backout play, 132–33
    screen and roll, 131
    shooting the gap, 130–31
Vulnerability of zones, 35
Vulnerable areas, 16

W

Wing cutters, 168–69
Wing-Denial option, 12
Wing-to-point pass, pressure, 114–15
Winning zone offense, 35

Z

Zone full-court press, three basic
    options, 96–98
Zone full-court press pattern, personnel
    alignment, 95–96
Zone offense:
    difficult plays, 31
    double-down continuity, 13
    dribble-entry play, 16–17
    fundamentals of, 35–37
    UCLA Entry Play, 13–15
Zone offensive series, 37–59
Zone-press assumptions:
    inbounds passes, 181–82
    penetration passes, 182–84
    scoring play, 184
Zone-press defense, inherent
    weaknesses, 79
Zone-pressure defense, counteracting,
    79
Zone-pressure offensive patterns, 79
Zone pressure strategy, 181
Zone overload, *See* Overload
Zone vulnerability, 35
Zoning with man-to-man principles,
    161–62